The Cosmic Energy Disc -
A Key to Higher Dimensions

Channelled by Joan Isaacs

Published by Cosmic Disc Publications
Printed by E.P. Lowe Ltd. Broadway, Worcs.
Copyright Joan Isaacs, 1994

The wind blows wherever it pleases;
You hear its sound,
but you cannot tell where it comes from
or where it is going.
That is how it is with all who are born of
the Spirit

John 3. v 8. Jerusalem Bible

Acknowledgements

My grateful thanks to:

Diana for her light,

Cynthia, an excellent networker,

Eileen and the Evesham Group, for their recognition,

Barbara and the Malvern Group for their encouragement,

Jane, for her proof reading,

Barbara and David for their insight,

Shabra and John-Martin, for their organisation of the text,

Helga for her generosity, also Rosemary and her
        anonymous friend,

Diana L who was the first to see it,

Andrew for his enthusiasm

and to all those others who showed their
        instant recognition and love.

With Love and Light,
        Joan.

Introduction

From an early age, I have always believed that my life would contain some main area of work, or service. Lately I had come to the conclusion that this work had seen completion. I was a serious child, given to much day dreaming and fantasy. Brought up within a religious framework, it was not surprising that I wanted to dedicate my life to God. I entered an enclosed Order in my twenties and took my final vows, remaining there for twelve years. My spiritual life seemed dormant. I realised ultimately, that this was not the place where I could serve either God or my neighbour, so I made the painful decision to leave.

After much soul searching, I decided to train for Social work. It was within this setting I spent the next twenty-one years, mainly specialising in child care. Taking early retirement, I spent the next couple of years working as a hypnotherapist. Offering counselling and healing, I imagined that this must now be the main area of life work. My desire to serve others seemed to grow stronger. It was in 1981 that I became fully aware of my psychic abilities. My spiritual core saved me then from many uncomfortable situations. It was during this period that I channelled the higher self cards, depicting Chakra and energy levels in bright primary colours. At the time I was not given to understand their true purpose so they were put aside until 1993 when their message became clear. During the interim period, I would often look at them, wondering what spiritual messages they carried.

It was in 1981 that I moved away from all friends and events linking to psychic and spiritual matters. I felt a great need to surround myself with my own space. During this period, I led an isolated dreamlike existence. My friends were those who were totally uninterested in esoteric matters. All the time, I had the odd feeling that I was surrounded by something or someone. My spiritual nature cried out for God and I could find him nowhere. I waited because I knew with certainty that something momentous was going to happen. I was happy just to be. My sleep at this time was immensely rich in contact with other worlds, other beings. I lived in my sleep state, all this time I was being guided taught, loved and nurtured by some unseen presence I felt totally cradled and fulfilled within it. It was at this point, that I began to relate to the Cosmos.

This sense of the Universal oneness began to grow within me as the months went past, as years lapped into other years. I began to ask what was it I was intended to do? Who indeed was I asking! There was no sign, no indication, no visible or outward contact. Then one day it happened. I was shopping when I felt something brush against my foot. On looking down, I saw it was a watch, a quartz watch depicting a blue butterfly, with the word 'Shiva' over it. I recognised the picture with amazing clarity. At home, in the book of eighty pictures, I had channelled an identical butterfly, above which the word 'Shiva', was clearly written. At that moment I heard a voice that said very clearly, "It is time to wake up Joan." I got myself home in a daze, hearing this voice again and again. How could I ignore such a powerful portent? I did indeed awaken from that day onwards. I recontacted old friends who pointed me towards new directional paths. New connections began to be made. All friends who now came to me appeared to share a common frequency. We had goals and aims in common. This was to assist the planet, to give light and healing to a stricken world. Twelve years had elapsed since the pictures had been drawn. No channelling had been given relating to the pictures. Now it was given, and in a language I felt was not my own. Technically this was the language of a scientific mind, which alas mine is not! The pictures began to circulate and were soon in demand by others. They began their work of raising conscious levels.

It was at this point that my own consciousness opened. I experienced strong moments of cosmic awareness. Everything and everyone appeared to be changed, even myself. It was as though we had entered into a new dimensional level previously unencountered. I felt a tremendous love for all living things. All was within me, I was in everything. Nature and I were as one. With this experience came knowledge of my own responsibility and future work within this incarnation. This was the reason I had come to Earth at this time and at no other. I had needed to wait until now to begin this contract of service. As my consciousness expanded so did my sense of responsibility. Then I experienced "Them" as they drew towards me in love and wisdom. I was never more aware of the growing link between myself and "Them." Although no names were disclosed or given, I knew they were not guides in the mediumistic sense of the word. These were pure Galactic beings or higher energies.

One day I awoke conscious of a coloured disc around my throat, lying just above the heart area. The colours were indescribable. The disc spun and oscillated. For three whole weeks we communicated. I told no-one. It was then that I felt impelled to draw the disc, to channel it as I had done with the previous pictures twelve years ago, then others could share this wondrous thing with me. I knew with certainty, I could not draw the Cosmic colour banding as this was non-existent in present third dimensional time. However I was encouraged to make some effort, and with their help channelled the new symbol onto paper and so the Cosmic Disc made its bow into our world. At first I was unprepared to do anything with it. Then one day I became aware that my own etheric Disc had disappeared. The only Disc I was left with was the Disc I had drawn.

At this point I showed the Disc to a friend. She immediately bonded with it. For her it appeared to pulsate and move. She asked for a copy. Then the Disc was printed on a small scale, circulating to others who loved and immediately recognised it. For all who used it, there were incredible results. Some of these were Space travel, out of the body experience, healing, love, release from previous emotional blocks, and opening of the higher chakras. Channelling on the use of the Disc then followed. As instructions for its use emerged, these were circulated to those who had begun work with it. The Disc, to use the words of the channeller, is "a particle of Cosmic energy." Its connections are tied to new Cosmic frequencies that are opening to many awakened souls. The main message of the light beings who have lovingly directed this Cosmic tool towards us is that we should amplify our efforts in sending out love and light to the planet;that the establishment of light centres should be set up for the direction and emission of this energy; that we should now realize our own spiritual nature and divine origin. The channellings together with the three Discs and other Cosmic pictures are seen as working tools that define such goals. The present channelling purports to assist many souls who are actively seeking their own guidance. **Instructions for Disc use and how it works should be read before use.** Cosmic tokens are powerful in opening to Fifth Dimension levels. Much of the present channelling sets out our main task in bringing healing to a ravaged world. We are to be the bearers of the new Cosmic light that is the Source.

Joan Isaacs
Mickleton
February 1994

Note Galactic Beings have communicated the present channelling,at times, different modes of expression or content are employed during transmission. This may be noticable to both channeller and reader when a different frequency or channel is employed. This is a natural part of the ongoing process.

Contents

We are giving you an opportunity to work with the new colour frequencies. These energies are Cosmic in origin, and have not been harnessed to third dimensional levels before. The time has come when you may touch into fifth dimensional states. There are those of you who will recognise the colour energy immediately. They will seem familiar. You have of course worked with these before, and they will make themselves known at higher self level. The colour contains frequencies of cosmic coding. When the code is entered, there is a transmission of fifth dimensional sound. This may fall upon the auditory system as vibrant sound. Do not be concerned if, at first, the higher frequency is not heard. The third dimensional ear is conditioned to receive acceptable sound levels, and the cosmic note may fall outside these levels initially. There will be a gradual shift in attuning to these different frequencies. At first you may hear visually! The coloured sound waves produce corresponding notes within the etheric body, these are absorbed and may only be brought into consciousness momentarily. This safeguards against undue shock to the nervous system and prevents throwing it out of balance.

Some of you may subconsciously register sounds you have heard before at Cosmic level but no longer recognise. The collective memory will have retained these. At conscious level they appear to be light-filled, promoting strong emotional release patterns. All this is to be seen as part of the process, working towards entry into the fifth dimension. Release from blocks of third dimensional encumbering creates a field for purification. Some of you will experience strong feelings of *déjà vu*. As this occurs, you will begin to recall and recognise former states when you were more closely aligned to the Source. A sense of home sickness combined with a desire to return is not uncommon. This is entry into the fifth dimension.

Linking to us during short transmissions will occur more frequently, becoming deeper. You will see us and we will change in our energy. The pictures allow you to channel us, and with continued usage stronger mind prints ensue. There may be some initial disorientation within the physical or emotional body at first. This will quickly correct, adjusting to more comfortable levels. The coloured light rays are in process of altering physical matter to receive them easily. See this as a preparatory step for fifth dimensional participation. We tell you that fear will retain you at third dimensional level. Move away from negative energy with all its myriad powerful man made thought forms. This energy is dark and must be released or dissolved before you travel forward into pure light. We are at hand to assist you in this purification. Let go of your heavy luggage; in doing so, you will gain Cosmic height. The opportunity has been given to you now. Do not reject it!

Some adjustment is necessary between left and right hand brain function. This is a temporary state. Alignment of both will ultimately balance out in total harmony. Equal polarity is requisite to this new channel. Touching in and out from third to fifth dimensional state will be gradual. We do this to protect your nervous system at all times. This eliminates excess jarring or jolting, easing your change of dimension, making it comfortable and enjoyable. To suddenly transfer from one state to the other would cause distress and even total disorientation. Do not over- amplify your energy levels. We are giving you small exposure, gradually and over a period of time. The information we will continue to present will always contact your higher self who remains in loving union with the Source. Our messages will in time be absorbed at conscious level. For those of you who have a high threshold of sensitivity, the ability to respond to us will be facilitated.

An ongoing linking with soul-kin is taking place at present. This is fifth dimensional. Those of you who are cosmically linked will re-unite now as never before. There will be great energy present in these encounters. You will experience extraordinary feelings towards your own soul grouping which will support and sustain you in these difficult times. You may experience great feelings of love, immediate recognition, unexplained moments of home sickness. As and when meetings take place within groups, there will be amplification of light and power. The light will pour out from your heart centres, illuminating the dark areas of this planet. Because of the increase of light within, you will find it necessary to discharge light to all within your path, friend or stranger. At times it will present as a great sword emitting powerful laser beams. There will be an increased sense of being part of all life. We are all one soul, we are all one light.

Given 18th May 1993

Picture energy comes through communication between the visual image and contacting the higher self or mind. The visual content is absorbed and recycled out at chakra level. The chakra stimulated will vary according to individual awareness and insight. The input of particular colour banding links automatically to the higher self, creating new channels of cosmic energy which when released create increased magnetic spiritual flow.

The new light energy helps to clear emotional blockages, leaving the meditator with a sense of deep inner peace and tranquillity. There may be an increase in awareness or sensitivity. As the new channel is repeatedly contacted existing soul light is amplified and empowered. Love and light are experienced in loving interaction, and being received, result in the outpouring of light particles or rays. The creation of this light assists in restoring and restructuring areas of dense planetary darkness that have existed for centuries born out of negative thought forms. The resulting lower Astral will be unable to sustain the penetrating power of these light rays that act as a laser beam to disperse and eliminate.

The pictures also link to cosmic or angelic beings acting as guardians and messengers. These pure light beings are strongly attracted to Earth at this important time and have drawn closely to us to assist and encourage greater spiritual growth. They see the metamorphosis of man in his final act of returning to the Source as both painful and beautiful. The soul looking within now sees with amazing clarity what it was and what it will become.

As the soul is now in the process of opening to new concepts, it is enabled to stand within the new light path having shed some part of that which previously held it captive. It is constantly being drawn into new dimensions of cosmic awareness. During this process, the physical part of man will become increasingly transparent, ever receding to allow for greater soul expansion until in his final dimension he is pure light and a permanent part of that cosmic whole from whence he came.

May 22nd 1993

You are looking at a particle of Cosmic energy that has been channelled. As you tune into the energy, visualise the format and interpret as before for energy transmitting pictures. Align with the colour frequency, which again is the coded entry into this dimension. Meditate with the colours until they appear to move or swirl. Such movement indicates transmission. Absorb the energy through the chakras, giving preference to the heart and higher chakras. Retain the energy at these levels for as long as is comfortable. The energy will remain within the etheric, serving as a link between inter-dimensional Cosmic levels.

When not in contact with the picture, use creative visualization techniques and picture the energy as a circular disc worn around the neck and over the heart area. Transmission will continue. Renew the flow of Cosmic energy frequently, breathing it in and out. Cosmic imprinting will ensue, improving physical, mental and emotional states.

The disc may change structure and rays of a single pure colour emerge, extending beyond the circle. This is in response to a positive bonding of the Cosmic Energy and will occur at times when additional energy may be absorbent. Almost always this is seen within the third eye. These new Cosmic rays bring the light beings into closer contact with you all now, strengthening karmic contracts or revoking them. We invite you to examine the workings of these new channels. Energy patterns are converted into symbols. The light frequency emitted by that symbol is dependent for translation at individual level. Unstructured patterning is a purer form of energy and is often seen before any recognisable imagery builds into accepted mind picture. All new energies are Cosmic in origin. In the final analysis, interpretation into the energy of the symbol presented depends upon recognition, and the individual's capacity to project it so that it creates its own Cosmic note.

Given 5th June 1993

When working with the Cosmic Disc, place it away from you at a reasonable distance, say three to four feet, on the ground or against a wall. Line the Disc up with the coloured centre at eye level.

It is important not to contact the Disc visually for more than one minute at a time. In any case, close your eyes immediately if any eye strain or discomfort occurs. Do not use the Disc more than once a day until we instruct otherwise. Cosmic Energies may present strongly at first. With continued use, they will moderate to more comfortable levels. The energy is laser structured, sending out beams of Cosmic Light. The coloured specks are tiny particles or pulses that are magnetic. They have the ability to absorb at fast levels.

Some of you may find, when looking into the centre of the Disc, that the colours appear to merge or pale to white. This is due to the spectrum rainbowed effect. Parts of the Disc may eclipse or fade completely. This implies that Cosmic energy is being absorbed into your chakras. Only the four higher chakras are able to meet this input. The ensuing result will be a cleansing or purification action, which when effected, allows purer Cosmic energy to be retained within the etheric. As you will ultimately become increasingly multidimensional, this process will facilitate the new channel frequency.

We are unable to experience your fear, so we come to you with great love and understanding. We hope to find that loving response and degree of trust within those of you who are cosmically linked and initiated. We offer you the opportunity to work with us through the Cosmic Disc. If you are able to accept this process, it will open the door to a new and beautiful dimension, which is your birthright.

Sharing this information implies increased discernment and greater responsibility. As Co-Guardians, you have a duty to care for and to protect the Disc at all times. Share its power only with those who are of your soul-grouping. In time we shall teach you how to heal with the Disc, sending its light over time and distance. Much of this new teaching is dependent upon your own trust and willingness to go forward. We send you much love and light for we are always close to you.

Given 17th June 1993

Increase and enhance Cosmic energy by absorbing it. Breathe it in. It is the universal air. The vibratory levels of this breath are higher than the normal oxygen intake, so there may be a sensation of over stimulation or some slight disorientation at first. There will be an increase at Crown Chakra level that may cause slight discomfort initially. Remember you are entering into a lighter frequency that is coming from the centre, the Source. You need to feel comfortable with this new energy and to accommodate it within your present earth form. What you receive is safe because it is fractional, a mere speck of pure universal light. You cannot assimilate more at your present third dimensional level. That is why we have sent you the Cosmic energy disc. It will assist you to extend your awareness and serve to link you to us more frequently. You will always be protected when using it to enter Cosmic space. The mode of entry will be gradual and returning made safe. The energy you will receive during these transmissions will resonate within your psyche, always raising spiritual levels. It is also a point of connection, a point of communion.

Look into and through the Disc with us. Your spiritual horizons will enlarge, a new dimension unfold. It is like entering through a door into another world where you feel held in a timeless moment of love. It is transparent space and time. The space you are entering is the womb of time where you were cradled in other worlds, other dimensions. It is a return, an assurance of what is in safe keeping for you. We carry you in our arms like small children. We hold you within the tiny bubble of Cosmic energy. You have been awaiting this next stage of higher consciousness over many of your incarnations. That moment is with you now.

You have a clear responsibility to carry the seed of this knowledge to those who will readily listen. Many are awakening at this present time. Some are lost, immersed within great blocks of negativity, imprisoned within their minds. Free them, set them upon the path that leads only in light to the Source. All are in process of returning. This is your particular time for service of a heroic nature. If you focus upon light, you will become that light. Look into the disc, absorb its powerful laser beam. You will then reflect and give back that light. Meditate after working with the disc; it will help you to focus more deeply, and to contact your higher self with increased awareness. Everything you require is within yourself.

The return of the Ancient Wisdom you knew so well, and which was the very fabric of your existence in other incarnations was never lost, only forgotten and replaced by increasing levels of planetary darkness. Your natural inheritance is returned to you so that you may use it now with greater love and understanding. It is the way back, it is the home-going. Again use the Cosmic energy disc to remember those other incarnations when you and the Earth were fused in a loving relationship of mutual harmony and trust. Many of you are searching for this path and will rediscover it. We shower you with love and light.

Given 19th June 1993

3 The use of this number indicates the slowing down of vibrational levels so that Cosmic energy may be seen within our third dimensional field of vision, presenting as coloured matter within a circular disc. As the energy enters Earth's atmosphere it is held momentarily at our level before re-absorption into the Cosmos.

6 This number indicates Cosmic wheel spin that converts back to original energies. This is often seen as transparent or colourless within the circular disc

9 Indicates Cosmic coding. When entered it will permit disclosure of Galactic information or data.

When all three numerals are invoked, they allow extended gaze-flight into the rainbowed spectrum. During this transmission there could be altered states of time and space. Departure from third dimensional time will be fractional and protected at all times.

Breathe the numeral chosen on the in breath. Tune into the Cosmic colour banding, at all times contacting the higher self. Invoke the Cosmic protection of the three Archangels, Michael, Gabriel and Raphael, during transmission, binding yourself strongly to them throughout. This act ensures that only spiritual cosmic beings will attract to you. Absorb the vibrational flow of the disc in love and trust. Remember, invoking different numerals links you to different frequencies or channels. Begin always with the numeral three. Stay with this frequency until you feel comfortable with the emitting energy. Proceed only to Numerals 6 and 9 when instructed to do so by your Guides. They will phase in to assist you during this new process. Do not hasten this programme, continued use will prove beneficial.

A profound spiritual experience will present and unfold as frequent Disc contact is made. It is at all times an instrument for contact at Galactic level and will link to us. The moment of weaving in and out of dimensional time will be fractional. It is seen as a preparatory step for what lies ahead. At all times it is an ongoing expression of our love, and proof that we are at hand protecting and assisting you in your journey towards the stars.

Over many incarnations, man has chosen to return to this planet, a jewel in the galaxy, giving preference to Earth, and seeing the conditions here as favourable to the Karmic contract he had agreed when returned to the Source. Now that the planet itself is in process of spiritual ascension, it will be unable to support life forms as they exist. All life as we know it will be changed, and the earth, eventually losing its gravitational pull, will return to become a new bright star within the Cosmos.

Before your own individual ascension there must be great change, for these times are critical. That is why higher information is being given to those who are cosmically aware. We always leave you with free choice, for you are free spirits. We surround you with great light and name ourselves as "The Galactic Brotherhood."

Given 19th June 1993

Using the Disc in a healing dialogue will formulate to advanced medical techniques. The knowledge we convey to you through your higher self will manifest in colour coded references and diagnostic information. Each colour frequency may be contacted for healing by a mind diagram. This intelligent communication works with those of you whose minds are opening to a new dimensional level.

The existing condition is showered literally with coloured light rays that absorb and disperse negativity, reinforcing positive polarities. By correcting the imbalances throughout Chakra and Meridian systems, and by surrounding the infected area with pure Cosmic light, we transmit rays that act as a powerful laser permanently restoring healthy functioning. Gradually the seat of the disease is penetrated and dissolved by the purifying action of this light. The receiver's vibratory level is enhanced and, as light pours in, his spiritual awareness increased as the heart Chakra opens to unconditional love. Use the new energies now encircling the Earth as a means to restore man to his original state.

Use the Disc as by the scrying method to look into the body, viewing dysfunction in colour. This will indicate as light or dark areas or as a single colour. Any obscurity will imprint upon the mind of the healer: it will seem as though you are looking at a screen indicating relevant information and data. This is new dimensional healing. Simply view the dysfunction and delete, just as you would correct a spelling mistake.

The healing process is often fast. Much depends upon the positive response of both healer and patient. The new light energies contain high frequencies. We have invited you to harness them in this programme. There must exist throughout treatment an ongoing telepathic communication between healer and recipient. The condition once diagnosed is received here as upon a Cosmic Screen and dealt with at a Cosmic level, by correction or deletion as appropriate. In effecting such a programme, you will find that your intuitional levels will develop and increase as you practise. Always remember the information you will receive from us is Cosmic in origin. We are allowing you to contact data at third dimensional levels for the present.

Practise holding the mind picture of the Disc at the third eye level. Enter the appropriate code and receive data. Transmit the information to both left and right hand brain polarities. Both will synchronize at integrated levels. Cosmic laser will discharge at frequency and colour, appropriate to individual requirement and treatment. Emotional thought blockages may be lifted out in totality, strengthening the cellular structure so that a regenerating process ensues. Magnetic flow to weakened meridian pathways will allow greater input of energy to depleted organic structure throughout. The end result is always greater mental, emotional and physical balance.

Our purpose here now is to assist in enhancing your spiritual vision. We imbue you with our light. We lift you up to the Source.

Given 26th June 1993

The magnetic and absorbent qualities of pure Cosmic Energy have frequencies faster than light and sound. They may be compared to another pulse beating at a different rate. The seat of this electric pulse may be detected within the physical and may be felt as a second heart beat. In the healing programme, the second pulse is always in tune with the healing process, automatically adjusting to the Cosmic life force. Our purpose here now is to purify and enhance your spiritual being. Once filled with Cosmic light, all impurities in the system are cleansed, allowing a clarity to penetrate the body that is light and transparent in nature. This purifying action may have been long delayed in many of you, and you are now being given an opportunity to work upon these areas. Unless healers themselves are filled with this new concept and increase in love and light, their attempts to heal others will be abortive. We are assisting you to "make whole" that which has lived in constant fear and darkness over many of your incarnations. How long have you awaited this moment in time? We imbue you with our light and enter into you in order to disperse, with your consent, that darkness and fear that leads to increased separation of the soul from the Source.

As we incorporate into you, our light will manifest to others. They will be aware of this soul-light and it will draw them towards you. Your healing is to be from your heart-soul-light always. The power we send must not be misused for personal pride or gratification. See yourselves as empowered to work on the highest levels for the good of all with whom you come into contact. This love is pure energy and is the medicine many are in need of at these critical times. We are permitted to return to you some of your original gifts, long lost over many incarnations, where you remained at the same level of development. You must honour these gifts; never abuse them or they will be lost to you forever. When the dark forces overwhelmed you they were removed to be held in safe keeping. Soul evolvement, now that it is in the process of moving towards the Source, merits once more the return of Ancient Wisdom.

Healers, you are the new light workers. Not only will you heal at new dimensional levels, you yourselves will be charged with an increase of power so immense that all will be suffused by its sweetness. The light is poured into pure souls who are becoming channels for those of us who have returned to assist the planet, and who heal by light waves that come directly from Solar systems many light years away. As many are enlightened and now stand within this new light, they are allowed to assist us in the work of transformation. All your previous information regarding healing, indeed all orthodox healing methods you have committed to mind, will be useless to you. Our teaching implies levels of evolvement able to tune into new dimensional skills.

Given 27th June 1993

The energy you have seen within the Cosmic Disc represents the new energy now encircling Planet Earth. It is the Christ consciousness. It will pierce and destroy planetary darkness and lift you to Universal peace and light. This new energy is sent to you at a time when your world is at crisis point. As you begin to understand the beautiful process of metamorphosis that is taking place, you will be changed; transcending your earthly sphere. We ask you to participate in this transitional process.

Third dimensional time is fast running out. Your glorious destiny is to become fifth dimensional and ultimately pure light. In this increasing evolvement of soul consciousness you will become the Christ Light. All those who aspire to this enlightened state will ascend and be transfigured. These souls will not be lost, for they have accepted us in love and trust. No matter what lies ahead, events cannot touch or harm you. You have chosen to be the elite, the God-vessels. The disc is a token sign. We send you the rainbow in the heavens, sign of God's love for you. We are part of Him who is the source and we serve Him with our whole light beings. Bond to us, work with the Disc, make it known to others. Practise the programmes we have entrusted to you through the channellings.

The Disc has both input and output. Each carries a different frequency or channel. The user receives at individual level that which is requisite. The input works to advance Cosmic awareness. The energy, both refining and purifying, is received by the higher self, sometimes strongly imprinted, at other times subtle and gentle. The output absorbs particles of negativity, which over time have clogged the purity and entry of Cosmic consciousness. Clearing these old genetic patterns from the DNA releases a strong healing flow which increases physical, mental and emotional well-being. The output channel is magnetic, removing from the DNA genetic encoding that which over time has become thick, eroded and distorted, so that it has prevented entry of soul-light. As the new energy penetrates old genetic patterns, the DNA is cleared, allowing light frequencies to enter the body which promote healthier functioning, this coupled with the soul's growing desire for increased contact with the Source.

There is always some recognition when looking into the Disc. This is because you are reconnecting with your soul as it emerged at the dawn of time, pure bright innocent and full of light. Your nostalgia reminds you of the growing separation from this original state. You are now empowered to step again into the light of that first dawn, and to recreate by patterns of self healing and love that former experience of pure Christ light. You may experience difficulty at first. Emotional blocking may be present initially when working with the Disc. This is a temporary state and will clear to a quiet and peaceful ongoing dialogue. As the old DNA structure is pierced, a sense of well-being and healing are then experienced. Remember at all times that it is your own responsibility to evolve spiritually. Everything you need is within you. We are here to assist you.

<u>Given 4th July 1993</u>

You have begun work with the Cosmic Disc. It is now at the point of linking and bonding to you, establishing an input within your higher self. We would like to help you send out the disc in love and light to Planet Earth.

As you tune into the Disc on a daily basis, you will experience during your meditations an increase in spiritual awareness. This, coupled with heightened sensitivity, will lead to powerful shifts within the heart chakra, so that an abundance of light and love ensues. This may present as a gradual building process as you continue to bond with the Disc.

There will be strong desires to share Disc energy with others, and you will experience the wish to send out the Disc as new waves of light and love permeate the heart chakra. Using Creative Visualisation techniques will enable you to practise Disc send-out. Engage the Disc and absorb it into the heart chakra on the count of three or six. Breathe in through the nose and out through the mouth. Always begin the count on the in breath. Create the mind picture of a large rainbowed Cosmic bubble. See it being sent out by you with unconditional love. See the bubble getting larger, increasing in size always dependent upon the strength of your love ray. See it floating away from you into the sky, carried by the winds and coming finally to rest somewhere within the planet. You send it to where you wish it to travel, creating mind magic for the journey.

Imagine this Cosmic bubble coming down to earth full of love and light. It rests in a meadow. The earth is parched and dry, there has been no rain for some time. The grass is brown and dry. Meadow flowers withered. Large cracks run across the ground's surface. Animal life search for water and find none. As you look there is a wonderful transformation all around you. As the rainbowed bubble makes contact with the earth, it revives and restores everything within its radius. The grass springs up tall, rich and green. Flowers blossom again with greater beauty and fragrance. Insects and animals scurry to drink fresh pure water. The light of Cosmic rays have penetrated the earth and healing has taken place. Balance has been restored. You have sent out your love and light. What you send to the Planet is never lost, rather received and taken up.

Send out the Disc again. This time the rainbowed circle appears to be larger. It is because you have sent out an increase of soul-light, and we have joined to you. This time the Disc finds its way into a house. You see it entering the house. It finds its way into the heart chakras of all living in that house Then it shines powerful light rays into their hearts. As they receive the light, experiencing unexpected warmth, their response to one another shows a marked increase in love. Their hearts open like flowers. They too have received what you sent out.

This time the Disc is sent out to a crowded street. The rainbowed bubble in seen entering the hearts of people hurrying along. They too begin to feel love, smiles and greetings are soon exchanged. All go their separate ways, carrying the light. As they journey homewards, that warmth in the heart chakra is still there. They do not know how to account for it, nor do they wish to lose it. You have sent out love and light, you have planted a tiny seed of Cosmic origin. What you send out cannot be lost. You are healing the planet. You are replacing darkness with light. The present Karmic contract will be appreciably lessened by this work of silent healing. This is the time for extraordinary acts of love towards your fellow men. Be bold, even outrageous in your thinking. These new energies are held in trust for you at a time when the earth is becoming increasing unstable due to the sheer madness of mankind. You are the new guardians of the earth. You are the new transformers. You are the light carriers. There is nothing, ultimately, except love and light. That is all you should send out now, to correct and rebalance negativity. If you send out negativity, in this present climate it will breed voraciously. Be the light, extend the light to the darkest corners of the Earth. We surround you at all times with great love. We are all one soul. We are all one light.

Given 7th July 1993

Some concern has been expressed regarding the channelling on input at higher Chakra level. How is it possible to work only with the higher chakras, giving less credence to the lower centres? Over stimulation of the higher Chakras could lead to disorientation, or even imbalance. We would like to emphasise use of all centres within the spiritual body of man. Although the heart Chakra is the main input-output for the Cosmic Disc or rainbowed circle, corresponding Chakras are always involved.

The heart Chakra is the balancer or fulcrum for all others. It is symbolised as a tuning fork or conductor which aligns and tunes every centre, ultimately producing a single cosmic note which is full orchestration. The love-light energy, emanating from the heart, creates an energy flow which aligns and rebalances both higher and lower chakras. The Disc contains the total spectrum of colour in rainbowed energy which, permeating in ever increasing flow to each centre, covers them with spiritual light and love.

The heart Chakra, being in total balance, then stands within the light of the spiritual sun, maintaining healthy balanced flow. There is always constant movement and spin; there is no need to open or close these centres mentally. The heart light energy ensures rebalancing and alignment automatically. Think of a never ceasing upward and downward spiral emanating from the heart centre, descending and ascending, always returning to its original point. To interfere with this natural movement would result in a blockage which cuts off important energy to that centre. Any previous imbalance has stemmed from the heart centre and affected both higher and lower chakras. Once the heart Chakra has been awakened to the Cosmic Sun, there is free and unblocked flow from and to all other centres.

Attempts to raise Kundalini energy from the base to crown Chakra has been practised over many centuries. At times this method has proved to be somewhat laborious, with little success, by many of you who may feel you have failed to aspire to this evolved state of soul development. Some of you have burnt out vital nerve centres and have become unbalanced or disorientated in the process. The time is here now when we would like you to practise a new way to increase in soul-energy. Concentrate by looking into the coloured Disc at heart Chakra level. Absorb the coloured particles into the centre. There should be no intentional created mind visualisation of separateness within the system, no colouring of chakra centres in separate primary colours. This picture is to be constantly replaced by one of merged spectrum rainbowing and experienced wholeness and totality. The old knowledge of different coloured centres, running from the base of the spine to the crown of the head, should be discarded entirely. This will only block and dilute new powerful energies, prohibiting full expression of total Chakra output within the spiritual body. Visualise a double spiral, beginning and ending in constant ceaseless flow from the heart centre, replenishing both higher and lower centres. It is only then you will experience increase of soul-energy.

N.B. There should be one single reference and that is to the Spectrum contained within the Cosmic Disc which includes all known third dimensional colours. These are seen within the disc as coloured particles of energy. Fifth dimensional colouring will appear as white. As this programme is a powerful way of harnessing Cosmic energy, and of awakening the Chakras, do not attempt to over use this exercise during the initial changeover period.

Given 9th July 1993

Cosmic rays emanating from the rainbowed Disc stimulate mental activity, promoting an increase in wholeness, which serve to enlarge spiritual and physical well being. The Disc may be harnessed to self-healing programmes. The particle component of Cosmic energy is linked to the Source, or Cosmic wheel of life. This two fold communication is inter-dimensional. Ever flowing, ever replenishing. There is no diminution in this ceaseless tide which is constantly returning and returned from the Source. The living energy is both pulsating and resonating.

As co-creators you have powerful access to this source of boundless, unending energy. It is rather like switching on a light switch. You may not understand the process of the connections which enable you to use this resource. What you have understood is that it is there, so you merely switch it on and use it. With man-made systems, there is always breakdown and malfunction. If a fault presents, energy is prevented from reaching you, although all the connections are still there. Correction of the fault enables energy to resume flow. Cosmic energy is a natural source always available to you. You simply tune into the frequency and switch it on. The more you attune and align with this source, the stronger it becomes. It is a channel.

Remember we told you in previous channelling that the Disc has both input and output. Both are utilised in a self healing programme. When you attract Cosmically charged light particles, the resulting energy is enormous. Its amazing power triggers sympathetic vibratory levels within the organism. The frequency of Cosmic ray travel is like a perfect rhythmic wave pattern, entering your bodies to correct former imbalance. Restoring former patterns within the DNA of improved health.

Colour therapy in the past has separated colour rays and interrupted vibratory input. This has diluted treatment programmes. We ask you to harness the total rainbow circle or spectrum for all future healing. Visualise waves of pure Cosmic light, projected through space as powerful lasers, being distributed and absorbed through the Cosmic Disc which is the connecting point, creating harmonious vibrations of peace and harmony into the etheric body. This is a recharging and revitalising process. By tuning into the colour waves, an expansion of Cosmic consciousness takes place, which is flawless. Cosmic light is creative, vital and self healing. It attracts perfect health, wisdom and balance. You are in a sense returning to that first primal creative light and being, replenishing yourselves in the radiance of inexhaustible Cosmic light wave frequencies which maintain all life, and which are centred at the Source.

Self healing programmes, by the use of colour and light, not only open the gateway to an increase in self awareness, but restore imbalance by correcting faulty DNA function. The Disc has magnetic qualities which when coupled with your magnetic aura, form a circuit of balanced negative and positive polarities. This then acts to clear, correct and rebalance zones of negativity which have bred the symptoms of impaired health. A new pattern is established which is creatively and positively charged.

Given 10th July 1993

The disc will vary in the amount of energy it discharges. Initially, there may be strong output. This may present at changed levels after the first encounter. No two individuals will receive the same experience, as all souls are at different levels of evolvement. The energy it discharges will always be present, matching individual soul-growth. Energy is sometimes transmitted as quiet and comfortable input. Daily use of the Disc, followed by short meditation, will enable stronger bonding to ensue. Gradually the image of the Disc will be retained at mind level without looking at it. Ultimately it will be seen visually, whenever Cosmic light and energy are requested. The soul begins to remember the light of the Cosmic dawn and because the memory of this assists in its present purification, it will be strongly drawn to recreate that original state. The Disc plays the role of connector.

Much depends upon individual soul development, or soul strengths. Often, energy levels may fluctuate. Just as your days vary with events and you are affected by them, so the resultant communication with the Disc may change in input-output. The changeless energy of Cosmic light is, however, unaffected; its source is endless, although it will only discharge what you are able to absorb. At other times the Disc will give out different signals. These may indicate temporary blocking, indicating areas on which you need to work. The higher self will always receive such information, although the choice to accept rests with the individual.

Disc input is always received by and through the heart Chakra, which will increasingly open to love and light, drawn towards it, irresistibly. Negativity will recede as it cannot bear to stand within this ever growing light source. We stand in your time and send you much love and light for your final journey. You are returning to the Source; many of you will not choose to incarnate again.

Given 12th July 1993

The absorption of colour rays is necessary for the building and continued nurturing of the Cosmic light body. It is the vehicle for extended soul travel. Being translucent and composed of finely textured rainbowed light, it is not visible at conscious mind levels. Its housing is within the etheric, which when saturated by Cosmic energy rays will expand and continue to increase dimensionally until it touches fifth dimensional time. The Coloured Disc is one way of contacting and aligning to Light Beings who are willing to incorporate into you now. They imbue the circular disc with stardust energy particles which, when taken into the etheric, are absorbed by the DNA.

Initially the input will not register at conscious levels. Gradually, however, there will be a noticeable change, manifesting as sharp increase in energy. Whenever contact with the Disc is made, this energy will transfer to the etheric. Teaching with the Disc in groups leads to greater amplification. The main work with you at present will be carried out during sleep. At times there will be experience of new sleep patterns. Deep and often dreamless. At other times increasing awareness of Cosmic travel, or contact with soul groups who occupy the same frequency channel. This is the chosen time to effect structural change which creates the new light body.

This body, being joined to the Universal Source, now finds greater attraction to link with that part of its nature which is spiritual. This bonding overrides all material considerations, which in the past have played so prominent a part. The journey back to the Source has now gathered speed. It is being accelerated. This is expedient as cataclysmic events are imminent. The new light body is the ascending spiritual soul-component which has remained constantly united with the Source.

As beings of pure light, we are now joined to your energy, and by carrying out this programme, we are helping to create spiritual expansion. We are the Universal consciousness. Touch into our light rays and you will be transfigured. This light energy force moves you ever upwards. It is magnetic, attracting and penetrating patterns of inherited DNA which have pulled you down to dense earth energies. We are the Creators of the New World, the new planet which is radiant with the light of spirit. This energy shift will affect everyone. All will be caught within its powerful impact. At times, many of you will experience unprecedented lightness of being. Your physical bodies will also be affected as the increase of light rays make themselves felt even at conscious level. You will "Soar like eagles." In the time span allocated to you, learn how to harness and work with this new light source. Incorporate into your hearts the knowledge of the Ancient Wisdom. It is your birthright. Learn to recognise fear as the only force which separates you from this new dimension of love. Create new patterns of trust and openness, and go forth in that armour which is totally protective, even in the face of events which will shake your faith to its foundations. Your shield is the ever increasing knowledge that all these things will pass and that your glorious destiny is towards the stars.

Given 16th July 1993

Use of the Cosmic Mandala links directly to the DNA and cellular structure. Use the same procedure in looking at the Mandala as the instructions for working with Cosmic Disc (see channelling). The time sequence for absorption should be about one minute. Use of the previous numbers, three, six and nine, will facilitate full Mandala information. This input will be faster. The energy will circle around head, throat and heart chakras. The purpose of ingoing energy will promote purification and cleansing of existing faulty DNA patterning.

Many of you may experience an uplifting of energy which opens to a higher level of consciousness. The input may present strongly initially, as with the Cosmic Disc. As you work with the Mandala, more comfortable levels are established. The Heart Chakra will experience an increased energy, opening more widely to love and soul-light. The main colours of Pink, Green and Yellow activate heart and throat centres especially. Energy may be felt as tingling or slight pressure in or around these opening centres. Your consciousness is already expanding and you are in the process of genetic and cellular change which is preparing you for fifth dimensional ingathering.

As you begin to experience the light which is entering in you, you will find that you are functioning at healthier levels, that there is a recognizable increase in energy levels. This is due to restructuring of eroded DNA which has held you back over many Earth incarnations. The freeing of this restrictive chain-like structure enables you to breathe freely, entering into fuller participation of the Cosmic experience. It is rather like a prisoner who has been fettered by heavy chains for a long time, held captive in a dark place, finally emerging freed into the light.

We have to ask you once again for your continued trust. Fear or suspicion holds us back. It is darkness to us, we cannot come close to you where these dense vibrations exist. We are able to assist you in your transition to fifth Dimensional space-time. With our help and love you will be enabled to make the adjustment necessary. Look once again at the Mandala after reading this channelling. It will be translated at mind level as a picture which shows you very clearly the freedom of the soul, purified, full of pure love, making its personal Ascension, and ultimately returning to the Source.

Given 19th July 1993

There are those souls who are unable to interpret our channelling. This is because their vibratory level is still at the old level. Their light input is fractional and so there exists a state of soul which is heavy, carrying past conditioning programmes. This in turn sets up a chain like response of negativity which prevents entry of the Light Rays. They will find the messages too technical, or too advanced. They will make no further effort in this direction. We want them to know that it will be enough for them to work with the Disc in trust and love. It will teach at inner levels without need for words or explanations. The result will be true imprinting at heart chakra levels. The residual light energy will work to dispel darkness and fear, creating patterns of well being and light. Fragmentation will give way to wholeness. Healing will take place, and then these souls may participate in the spiritual ascent. If, after this, you find there is continued atrophy or lethargy, your responsibility in this direction is complete. Continue to send them light, although tempered with the realisation that they may not choose to evolve further at this stage. You are not accountable for them.

Realise that the true self is pure, perfect, untouched by the events of life, totally unconditioned and free. It is continually joined to the Source and after life there is true understanding of that union. It is the soul life which aspires always towards the highest good. The human vehicle obsessed with temporal time eclipses its light and dwarfs its development. Some souls never advance in any incarnation, choosing to remain at the same level of evolvement. They are never free, never realise wholeness. The chance to reincarnate has been afforded to them in the past, again and again. This opportunity for soul growth may no longer be afforded or, if offered, will not be on this planet, which is itself in the process of orbiting. They may find themselves on a similar planet which provides for Karmic purification.

You are in the process of emerging from earth bound Karmic contracts. The story of the caterpillar and the butterfly represent the ongoing process of metamorphosis in which you are presently engaged. The earth bound creature dreams of air borne flight in sleep, moving in its coils to simulate this. Then it is in touch with its wings and moves upwards. The dream has become reality. The earth casing is left behind, discarded, of no further use. You are spiritually ascending. You are finding you have wings! There are those of you already moving upwards, experiencing the initial stages of 5th Dimensional levels.

Much of previous earth skills and knowledge will be discarded now, their input will be useless. As your minds open to truth, you will discover there is no biological explanation for the increasing changes which are taking place. There will be a gradual realisation that a transformation has been effected. Souls exchanging with like souls carrying this new light energy will merge and become part of one another, the communication often without necessity for words. In this way you will become multilingual. Many souls will walk away from you. They will be unable to tolerate the light which surrounds you. We tell you again, you have no responsibility towards these souls, apart from sending them the Universal light. You do have however a responsibility towards your own spiritual evolvement. Once that is undertaken, there can be no turning back. You have made a new contract, and one that commits you to go forward at all times. It was said of the Master Jesus that "Who for the joy that was set before Him, endured the Cross." We cannot promise you joy fully in this world (although at times you will taste it strongly), only in the next. We are here at all times to help and assist you. We send you love and light.

Given 26th July 1993

Breath is the intake connection for Cosmic energy. By breathing it in, you draw to yourselves that which vivifies, animates. By breathing out, you are expanding into Universal time and space. This conscious exercise leads to an increase in Cosmic awareness. What you inhale-exhale is the total sum of living experience. The knowledge which now comes to you is a new conception of wholeness and being opening to new dimensions. It is creating the light body which depends for existence upon perceiving that which is intangible, growing from the spiritual tree whose branches touch the Universal heaven and whose roots are firmly in the earth. You have the climate of present time which offers you a fertile soil in which you are able to expand and grow, moving purposefully towards your spiritual destiny.

You have lived within the Universe, part of the Galaxy, over many incarnations. Asleep, unaware of the frequencies surrounding you. Had you been aware of such frequencies in the past, you would have been able to harness them to your own advantage. There have been many different energies for your use had you chosen to absorb them. As the Cosmic breath is now being experienced by many of you, it brings you into alignment with the Universe as a whole. Your own part in this unfolding evolution is clear to you for the first time since the dawn of man. One living pulse, resonating, vibrating, of which you are a vital component part. We are all linked to the Source, therefore our identity and your own are the same. Merging as you are now with Cosmic frequencies, or energy levels, implies greater clarity and discernment, also a growing sense of responsibility to all life forms as you know them.

Man has taken much from the planet; it has become depleted, exhausted. Plundered by its predator, life is running out, apart from the existing natural cycle which is also weakened. Man has become a warring machine, the destroyer. Instead of living closely to Earth, he has grown away from nature and himself. As this process continues, and unless man is spiritually changed, there is little hope for Planet Earth. His rapacious nature precludes ongoing evolvement. Constantly outside himself, he is no longer in tune Cosmically. Mother earth, or Gaia, stimulated and increased ancient wisdom in earlier days. Man is now a driven, restless creature, spiritually, mentally and emotionally declining. The redressing balance rests within himself: by listening to his own frequency or Cosmic note, there is realignment. He is at once part of the resonating Cosmos which brings him into focus and balance with his spiritual nature, his true self. What he needs to rediscover is that everything he requires is within. Isolation from this knowledge leads to ever widening gaps between himself and the Universe he inhabits, his original energies dissipated, diluted, rendered ineffectual by the artificiality of the world he inhabits, a shadow creature living in the half light of his own dread and fear. Man will only awake from his present torpor if he emerges as the spiritual giant he was intended to become; this will take place when he is joined to the Cosmic light, united finally to his source.

Given 28th July 1993

Cosmic light is streaming into each one of you now in ever increasing flow. You are connecting to the God-light in a very directional way. This results in the creation of the light body, which is radiant, translucent and powerfully vital. It is supercharged with energy which, when absorbed by the higher and lower subtle bodies, increases harmony, bringing man into sustained contact with his true self. In this light of increasing self awareness, power, in the form of light particles, enters and clears eroded DNA structures, promoting patterns of self healing. Inherited programming in the DNA has set up many blockages in the past which have created dense negative impedance. This has created a self protecting, defensive system, preventing maximum energy flow to the subtle bodies, rendering them ineffective and sterile. Neurosis, together with impaired health, have been the legacy of such malformed DNA functioning. As light enters, it clears the cellular structure, empowering and restructuring new energy flow which reaches powerfully into the body, creating higher vibrational levels. Cosmic light works to heal physical density, allowing body cells to separate, thus creating finer spacing, which is then filled with new regenerated cells which are produced at a purer finer level.

This process promotes new energies which recognise and permit closer integration of physical and spiritual bodies, allowing for expansion, and combining towards wholeness and well being. As you are saturated with the light so you will be able to direct your light towards others. It will pass through you to them, entering the emotional body. This channelling of light particles is effortless, causing no depletion as it enters. The source is inexhaustible. As you transmit to others, it is a process of send-return energy. Healing with light promotes an even flow. Create openings for the transmission of light Remember, others will only receive the light entry as they permit it. This energy always connects to the higher bodies initially, creating an increase of light which flows from higher to lower, nourishing and regenerating, erasing patterns of resistance it may encounter.

We are working with you at this time to help you find harmony and balance. There will be increasing alignment as you begin to get in touch with your inner selves. Your bodies are registering change at this time. Do not be alarmed; change is necessary for the structuring of the light body. Many blockages must be exposed and removed before you are able to enjoy the freedom and power of this new body. See change as integrating the physical with the spiritual. Your ascension is ultimately to merge with that pure light which is your final dimension. We send you love and light.

Given 30th July 1993

We have in previous channelling explained to you how the Cosmic Disc may be utilized in various ways. As it is composed of electromagnetic energy, it will under certain conditions produce a strobing effect which may induce altered states of consciousness. Resting within an altered state may facilitate the recognition of Ultra Sound. This song of the spheres is beyond the human ear range at normal conscious levels. The energy spots or coloured particles of the Disc surface, being magnetic, will act as a wave guide, tuning into the main transmitter which is the Universe as a whole. When the coded messages are received by the sensitive part of the human brain, contact is made and access admitted. This process enables more accurate tuning to take place, thereby establishing a valid connection. The Disc is seen as the component maintaining linkage between man and the Cosmic Galaxy, of which planet earth is an integral part.

Meditation with this aim in mind serves to bridge the gap between you and ourselves. Disc gazing opens a door in the psyche which bonds our worlds together in ongoing realistic dialogue. This energy fires man to seek more positively his true self and nature. Called the state of enlightenment by advanced souls in the past, and open to the

SECTION OF CROP CIRCLE ENERGY

select few, this door may now be entered by many. Communication between human and planetary consciousness makes this possible. Communion of souls on this frequency have direct understanding of all matter which is ever interconnected, evolving, living and resonating. This leap in consciousness has already taken place in many of you. This is because there has been acceleration. For many of you it is your last earth incarnation. It is vitally important for man to remake an ongoing meaningful relationship with the world in which he lives. This implies man is reconnecting to his spiritual nature, which is immortal. Only then will he be able to see himself as he really is, his true spiritual status accepted, only then will he be enabled to complete his journey, returning to the Source, enriched, raised up as the co-creator he was intended to become.

The artificial intelligence man is creating eclipses his true identity, taking him further into ultimate certain destruction. The return of man to the Ancient Wisdom, which he once practised, and which enabled him to live in the earth as its true son must be regained. Man's restless search will end only when he finally rediscovers himself. Then he will re-recognise his own world and participate in its terrestrial transformation.

We have your highest spiritual good at heart, that is why we are opening your hearts. The heart is the entry point. We have harnessed our light to your beings so that you may be illumined. In the final analysis, everything fades away, except love. You must learn how to grow in that fertile soil of the soul, work with the light energies of the Disc. You are moving towards Cosmic awareness at a faster rate than at any other time in evolution. We stand in your time to assist you.

Given 1st August 1993

The strobing effect of the disc emulates the resonating Cosmic heart beat. The heart is the central vibrating core of the Logos. Within the logos lies the Cosmic nucleus, source of world order and intelligibility. The nucleus, which is ever evolving, sends out intermittent impulses which radiate frequencies. This ever replenishing cycle regulates and distributes energy to all living matter. It regulates growth and movement, aligning and interacting to all within its form field. All life is contained in this cycle of continual Universal law and order. The repetitive cycle constantly attracts and draws to itself matter which issues forth in embryonic form, returning to the Source at the end of each completed cycle. The centrifugal force has a single vibration or note which interacts with universal sound waves. This note resonates with multi-vibrational organisms, directing all towards the Cosmic nucleus. It is a send-return process and the ultimate return implies the completion of the evolutionary process.

Since thought is movement, movement is part of this ever evolving process, having neither beginning nor end. The ceaseless spiralling vortex of time and space is now, a single moment. Earth time is man measured, artificially counted against light and darkness, seasons and fruition. As the conscious mind of man unfolds, there will be a different understanding of time. The new dimension he is now entering will require spiritual understanding of Cosmic time and space. Spiritual energy is entering into each of you at this time of especial evolution. With the increase of this new energy the present vehicle for earth experience will be drastically altered or changed to meet these new conditions. The physical body is already in the process of replacing the mental rule of intelligence by the spiritual role of consciousness. This implies emptying out of past learnt behaviour, together with conditioned inherited patterns which have served to denigrate man to a lower evolutionary level. The resulting inrush of spiritual awareness will serve to heighten new levels of sensitivity, creating the new dimension we have touched upon. This process is already accelerating due to change in the Universal order.

As the third dimensional mind of man empties there may be initial disorientation. This is in part due to physical levels being involved in the restructuring process. The materialistic mid brain will give way to the higher brain, called into functioning, thus fulfilling future evolutionary processes. Man's present mind has been too closely linked to artificial intelligence, which has precluded spiritual freedom. The new consciousness works to restore a new being whose main objective is to live in harmony and balance with his world.

The new dimension will render all previous knowledge obsolete. This "Quantum leap" will be taken by souls who are already beginning to touch in upon their new spiritual energy and who are in harmonic vibration with the Universal pulse or heart beat. They will become increasingly light saturated and therefore enlightened. The change is irreversible, there is no return. Their inheritance will be the new planet which has also evolved and man will again walk upon the earth in peace.

Given 7th August 1993

Energy received from the Cosmic Disc makes an input at higher brain level. This area of the brain is linked to higher states of consciousness. Throughout the evolutionary journey of man, few have accessed enlightenment. Those souls who have realised this state of being have created their own field of resonance, which still finds a level in the residual energy released into the stratosphere. It has significantly contributed towards the viability of the earth.

This higher functioning of mind-body has lain dormant in many of you until now, unawakened. Now it is being activated, to create total transformation. The Disc is one of many ways to contact this sleeping mechanism. As the Disc particles are absorbed into the higher brain, they tune into a common frequency to discharge increased spiritual energy. Touching in as they do upon the genetic code, they act as a trigger or chemical agent promoting the flow of ductless glands which in turn control the Chakras. This action facilitates major channelling of mind and body which become increasingly sensitive to the signals received. A shift in awareness and heightened sensitivity is the final outcome of frequent Disc usage.

The main changes will take place in the braincore and the heart. As the body cells undergo subtle change, this will affect the lymphatics. New glands will need to develop as ongoing protection against harmful substances which could damage the present immune system. This protective system must change and develop to counteract future body invasion. Such changes will occur gradually and will only register as temporary body discomfort in many of you. For some there may be longer periods of ill health. All will undertake this major change and most of you will clear it. This is already taking place.

The energy you absorb is important. It must be of spiritual quality which in turn creates balance and a sense of well-being. If you absorb negative energy, you will experience physical lowering or mental depletion which if allowed to build, permits low energy levels to infiltrate. This could prolong the process of body change since the physical seeks to be in tune with the spiritual. The absorption of light rays are important. Negativity cannot withstand light. You must work to send out more light.

Cosmic rays now encircling your planet act as an energy output to facilitate this change or mutation which will birth the new species of man, one who is spiritually motivated and consequently in balance and harmony, not only with his own world but linking realistically to other worlds, other galaxies. The heart is seen as the main agent for this new perfected state. As it opens to increased love and light it will move upwards to a new place within the body, finally occupying the brow, becoming the new third eye. This will give rise to higher states of consciousness. The evolutionary ladder will open the door to new dimensions, linking man more closely to the Source. He will then fulfil his ultimate destiny as Co-creator. The Ancient Wisdom returning, will embrace him as a true son of Earth, affording him kinship with the Cosmic heart.

Given 8th August 1993

It will be necessary for you to re-read the previous channelling on the Chakras. At this time especially, due to structural body change, there should be no intentional mind closing down exercise of individual Chakra centres. The electric body promotes a constant healthy flow of these centres at all times. They could be compared to a train following a familiar route which connects to various stations. Breakdown affects the entire system. Thought which curtails the natural energy within these centres, disturbs the balance of ongoing flow by projecting mind instructions to "close" or "open". The ductless glands also aligned to the Chakra system are then affected. All centres should flow in balanced output. This stop-go programme does little more than to prohibit by thought. As your thoughts are energy forms, the sensitive system is affected, natural flow is checked momentarily and the connecting centres bulge or contract. This is like a hiccough to the entire system. Many unrelated illnesses stem from this practise. The breathing is also held in restricting muscles and other organs.

You are now in the process of opening to gradual body change, and the flow of ductless glands together with the Chakra system must not be impaired. As you move into expanded states of consciousness, all requires to be in balance and harmony. Do not attempt any kind of restriction at this critical stage in your evolutionary journey. It will only cause uncomfortable jarring or jolting to the nervous system and new energies will be unable to be absorbed at reasonable levels Remember at all times the delicate connections between differing systems. All must flow as a whole, balance will be made automatically. You are always in control of situations and the increasing use of discernment will protect you from the dark forces. Always ask for protection, never assume it. As we channel this information to you, we want you to touch in upon the natural flow of the body. Breath in deeply and in breathing out, you will have increased the electromagnetic flow, increasing vitality.

We have already told you that the two main areas of change will involve the heart and brain area. Once activated, these open the pathway to higher states of consciousness. This will occur at a natural level. We ask you to consciously open your hearts to increasing love and light. As you do this, discernment will increase, allowing you to see with your heart what needs to be accomplished for the present and future. The heart is the largest field of energy and centre for the true Self. Energy from the heart rises to the crown chakra, descending again to the heart as a fountain of light. As consciousness moves from the heart centre it becomes a spiritual energy centre of pure intuition. It is the heart which finally unites with the Source. The heart must be the input area for the new energy. If it is received at any other level, it could fragment and fuse the delicate balance of the mind-body structure. The heart acting as a safety fuse protects against breakdown or disruption to the total mechanism. It becomes the valve of true knowledge and discernment.

<u>Given 9th August 1993</u>

The body chalice is the total offering and dedication of man to his Source. Cosmic awakening or awareness brings about body-mind integration at higher levels of consciousness. When man stands in his rightful place within the light of the Cosmic Sun and sees himself as a living part of the Solar system, he becomes totally immersed, part of the evolving universe. This is enlightenment. We are at the central point of the Cosmos, having never left or moved away from that incarnating womb. Only time has changed to a temporary state, so that man may experience all that concerns his true spiritual nature. This is called earth dwelling, and is a second in infinite time and space. Man, although outside time, is always returning to the Source because here is his true permanency and residence. He is for the most part unaware of these points of return, except in "peak experiences" when he is truly participant. These Cosmic mind flowerings are but a transient breathing of Cosmic Fire.

Man has entered into a lethargy from which he seldom awakens. Apart from brief moments of complete knowing, he is concerned primarily with earth experience and cannot detach himself from its illusory powers. This spiralling vortex of temporal time is repetitive until he fully awakens. He becomes part of the illusion which he perceives as reality.

As Cosmic light is breathed into him, earth levels which have impeded soul strength recede. The planet is seen in its true light, a temporary abode, and one in which he is always in the act of leaving. He views earth experiences as a preparation for recall. He knows with certainty that nothing here can be possessed in any permanent time sense, since its true value is transient and always called into question. When man realises with Cosmic awareness the true nature of the Earth in which he is a temporary dweller, he perceives its true identity as that of a living evolving entity. Then he is aware of his responsibility as a co-guardian. Only then is the spiritual partnership appropriately recognised and discharged.

The light of the Cosmic sun will presently manifest upon Earth, visible to each one. As you stand within its powerful light, you will be reabsorbed, knowingly, into the centre which is the Source. All forms of life will be changed. If you have made the preparation, you will transmute into a wonderful new dimension of soul-light which will permanently free you from the heaviness of the body-vehicle. Only then will you recognise the eternal "now" which is timelessness, sounding the Cosmic note which reverberates upon universal shores. As your consciousness expands, you will begin to experience and join with that permanent and true part of self which is constantly united with the Cosmos, This is the initial process of the returning journey which every soul must make. In great peacefulness and love, you will be reunited with your true self. In you final dimension you are pure light, reabsorbed into the Universal heart of the Creator. In this pure heart of love you will finally exist in timelessness, part of the single vibratory note which is the Cosmic resonating pulse.

<u>Given 10th August 1993</u>

Y ou began the evolutionary journey as a single cell which eventually, contracting with other cells, combined to create a multicellular organism. The original cell is the seat of being which contains, within its nucleus, predestined levels of individual evolvement. This Master cell is the original by which all other cells are governed and regulated. As such it serves as the main connecting point for soul-energy. Governed by Universal laws it remains constantly united to the Source, whence it emerged in embryonic form. The seat of its being is within the soul-heart area. From here it sends out its own individual energy or point of light, connecting to all created matter. This vibrational energy when transmitted to other energy forms, sets up electromagnetic waves which alter and affect the magnetic field. The mechanism is then either accelerated or slowed down by higher or lower vibratory emitted frequencies. This planet now is over saturated by slow energy patterns which have trapped natural energy, the result being that the body of earth which in itself is a living evolving entity is increasingly unable to discharge energy at healthy functioning levels. Pockets of light energy lie submerged, covered by the slower denser energy you humans have imposed and discharged into the stratosphere. More frequently this energy will seek to escape, surfacing in the form of floods, earthquakes and volcanic action. This is a natural outcome, where the earth is seeking to re-establish its balance and harmony. It is rather like producing a giant hiccough to restore equilibrium.

You must learn that the balance of your own dual nature, which is an ongoing alignment between higher and lower selves, is critical in sending out faster vibrational energy which will act as a healing agent, dispersing slower heavier energy pockets which have built up. This dense energy is acting as a suffocating blanket to destroy your planet. By sending out light and by generating purer energy, you may restore natural energy lines and systems which at present lie inert, poisoned and polluted. Only by fulfilling this will you be enabled to regenerate yourselves spiritually, since you are permanently linked to all living matter and consequently incur the same penalties. This is the natural law. It may be still possible for all to come together in love and light. Your present state of stagnant evolution is causing a downward spiral into the lowest levels. There are those of you who are now able to discharge a faster energy which is light saturated and therefore recuperative. This responsibility is recognised and understood by many souls at this present time. This is the emerging role of co-guardian. Know that the purer energy sent out by you is transmitted to the universal energy grid, and being received there is instantly

COSMIC PORTAL

re-transmitted to your planet. A recycling process. You will recognise this service to mankind and your planet as part of the original contract you undertook when re-united to the Source at the completion of your last evolutionary cycle. Uplift and touch many lives by sending out love and light, so that the holocaust may be averted. You are empowered by powerful vibrational energy at this moment in earth's time. Go forward in peace and strength.

<u>Given l2th August 1993</u>

Advanced technology, together with the increase of artificial intelligence, inhibits man's natural ability. As the former state prevails, man's intuitive level is lowered. This gross physical desire body eclipses soul strengths. As man searches for identity outside himself, he loses touch with his spiritual nature. Consequently his evolutionary ascent is negated, since he follows a road of materialistic values. Although this may afford him immediate gratification, it is nevertheless a temporary state, requiring ongoing reinforcement or replenishment to continue at satisfactory levels which meet long term goals. This state of being "outside himself" leads to increased dissatisfaction, as it inevitably links to events outside himself of which he is at times out of control. The resulting spiral of stress may ultimately induce physical dysfunction together with a growing sense of self dissociation. In this state man is asleep; spiritual atrophy ensues. . Release yourselves from the chaining mechanism of materialistic values. For many of you, the return journey to the Logos has begun. As your higher mind develops, there will be a shift from the astral body to the higher mental body. This transition involves the creation of another body, for use in a different sense, and on another plane. This is the light body; it draws from higher vibrational levels and is composed of finer energy. It is God-essence entering the world of matter being transfigured by the powerful light of the Cosmic Sun. This essence contains the seven colours of the spectrum. Know that all is energy is light returning to the Source. Know that all energy is vibrational in nature. Draw now upon these reservoirs of higher energy for the attunement of the light body. Become light conscious evolving souls.

The induction of colour and light is transmitted by the Cosmic Disc. The latter is vitally powerful in creating strong force fields which act upon the higher centres. As the inflow of energy is absorbed into the expanding consciousness, there will exist greater capacity to open to increased light waves. As plants and trees respond to light and finally flower, so your earthly vehicles will be light saturated, flowering in the light of the Cosmic Sun. This infusion of Cosmic light particles will cause electrons to fire in different sequence. Then linking to universal powerful radiating wave forms will act upon ductless glands, activating them strongly to effect structural change.

The colours in the Disc are designed to open the heart centre, to trigger higher planes of consciousness. Work with the Disc should be on a daily basis to ensure appropriate bonding. Breathe in the colour particles. They link to pranic energy which stimulates, raising vibratory levels. The Disc also works to nourish the auric field by increasing balance and vitality. Hidden within its spectrum are the new colours, as yet unrecognised by man. These will manifest in the future Solar system. They are already incorporated into the etheric. You may recognise these colours in altered states. They cannot be held in the mind at conscious levels yet. As your higher energy body is internalised, a quickening of the corresponding subtle bodies will follow. This process is inherent in the spiritual awakening.

Given l4th August 1993

Unless man is prepared to live on his planet in peace and harmony, unless there is a radical change in present attitudes, cataclysmic events are imminent. Armageddon will occur in the near future. Sea levels will rise with massive geological changes taking place. The increase in carbon dioxide will produce a greenhouse effect destroying the earth's protective layer. There may be massive radiation from outer space, due to a comet falling to earth. This will create a massive crater destroying most of the earth's surface. Gravitational thrust against axial plates will create planetary instability, resulting in powerful Galactic pull. The resulting tilt will lead to movement strong enough to pull the earth away from its natural orbiting cycle around the sun. If this takes place, the earth will be forced into a new magnetic path. Orbiting would bring it nearer to the sun and into the path of other planets within its radius. Proximity to the sun would generate excessive heat from the earth's core, activating volcanic action. There would be eventual decimation of all living matter. Humanity would attempt an exodus to other star systems, other galaxies. However, there would be little time to affect this. Add to this the fact that within the Cosmos there is already knowledge of man's warring nature. This factor would not predispose other Galactic beings to accept him as peaceful or to see him as validly contributing to their colonies. Man would find himself ousted from settlement in space or involved in lengthy wars to stake his claim outside the Earth.

There are other Galaxies, other Universes. Many are light years away, beyond man's reach. These are inhabited by beings, superior in the knowledge and use of energy, far advanced beyond the intelligence of earthmen. They have viewed the progress of man over time with increasing concern. Some of them have now elected to work with the earth for its healing and salvation. Their unchanging message is one of love and light. Because they are themselves composed of fine light energy, they seek to imprint that light into the hearts of men. Their message is urgently needed in a world where negativity gains increased hold. They are able to save your planet from terrible destruction. They stand in your time to save earth and to make it viable.

Look for them; they will make themselves known. They realise that the final choice rests with the individual. They are heard in the small, still voice within. As they are pure spirit, they have a resonance with all things spiritual. Clothe yourselves in their light, in their infinite wisdom. They come into earth space now, for they have chosen to do this willingly and with great love. They form the Galactic Brotherhood. These are the ascended masters. They impart true knowledge, the realization of man's true purpose and nature. Without their help, you would be given over to the destructive powers you have unleashed. All would rebound upon you in the most unfavourable way. Man must awaken to new dimensions which lead him into paths of peace. He must recognize his spiritual nature. Another Garden of Eden is then created, where he walks in peace with the whole Universal Galaxy.

Given 15th August 1993

There exists at present a battle between positive and negative energies. At this time the difference will register strongly. The light beings carry their light source into every corner of the Earth, seeking to disperse large built up areas of negativity. Where negativity has existed for thousands of years, it has formed into a solid mass. Once this mass has formed, it may be felt by sensitives as an alien energy. It is only dispersed by the opposite action of positivity. Able to remain in its present state until light touches it, it continues to affect those souls who are drawn towards its negative emanations.

You will begin to experience this negativity powerfully. This is because it is expanding, growing at accelerated levels. You will at times feel submerged by its hold upon you. This will call up in you, the need to become the light, to send out powerful laser beams of light energy to dissolve dark forces. This experience is necessary for you. Learn how to work upon those areas of self which are still out of balance and link to negativity. These manifest at physical, mental and emotional levels. Know that every situation attracts to itself either light or darkness. Your increasing discernment in these presenting experiences is critical. Work upon these areas now to clear them of negative residual energy which could inhibit light energy flow. It is only when you are clear from imbalance, that you may discharge energy at a higher vibrational level. We have previously explained how the lighter energy is purer and frees the light body, the latter acting as a healing agent to all evolving life forms. You, by discharging positive energies will strengthen the protective roof which shields earth from destructive neutrons impeding electrical flow. It is essential at this time to renew and strengthen this flow of natural energy which links the physical earth to the main grid network of the Logos. Any lowering of incoming frequencies could cause massive imbalance, with resulting cataclysmic disaster. This drop in vibrational levels will cause the network of earth's natural-supernatural balance to swivel into a new vibrational pathway, ultimately giving rise to a new planet or star.

Where ongoing energy supply is either interspersed or discontinued there will be an inability to supply continued input. This implies breakdown at main planetary network points. If this occurs, a slowing down effect will affect all life forms dependant upon incoming balanced energy. Cut off from its vital life flow, matter will cease to exist. Earth will then disintegrate, re-forming to create new planetary form within the Galaxy. By this process old worlds give rise to new within the Cosmos. Earth as a new star would have a new moon and sun within its solar system and a new orbiting path. All existing life forms would be eliminated. A new species of man would develop. This new species would move to higher dimensional levels. A spiritual man, able to live upon a new earth in peace and harmony, in balance with Universal laws. Unless your earth is healed, until negativity is dissolved, there is no hope for your future. Cosmic laws must be observed for planetary wholeness to ensue. The network of fast closing energy lines must be reopened and stimulated. Light must triumph.

Given 18th August 1993

The next phase will disclose man's new powers over natural and human worlds. Working towards the inclusion of mutated DNA carrying new genetic structure, man will be better adapted to a changing environment. This will be brought into existence by Genetic engineering. Controlled evolutionary growth will determine future mutational patterning. There are already changes to the DNA; this is occurring at natural levels as opposed to contrived artificial intelligence. Biochemical changes brought about by man to create a super species has dangerous implications. It gives rise to control methods by groups of unscrupulous men seeking maximum control, exploiting individual freedom. Such unspiritual groupings would be able to incept artificial chemical brain implants, creating a robotic man, who would obey slavishly, without choice or motive, and without super-ego strengths. This new semi-human could be used in many ways as a destructive agent, combining maximum strength of body and mind. The new species would be without spiritual insight. Artificial intelligence would supplant natural function. The dangers inherent in such futurist advances within the field of pioneering biochemistry becomes blatantly obvious. Materialism already rampant would increase to the detriment of spiritual values. Man would destroy his own kind in increasing numbers. Many souls will die as the result of germ warfare. Already laboratories hold lethal chemical weapons as alternatives to the destruction of cities or geographical terrain. These unspiritual groups seek to gain control of vast areas for their own devious ends. They are totally uncommitted to scientific progress which could benefit mankind. Countries will be emptied of natural riches and resources to satisfy their greed. Earth will cry out in pain as she is ravaged. Their rapacious spirit will enter into the hearts of Godless men, causing darkness and degeneration everywhere. Darkness will engulf the Earth.

Emerging as points of light are the healing guardians of the planet. They emit laser beams of pure energy which destroy negativity. Those souls who are aware of their spiritual task, to restore earth to its pristine brightness and light, join them. These co-guardians work within groups called "Light Centres." They amplify healing energies which rebalance planetary swerve. As more souls join these groups, the light sent out will powerfully ignite the force of love. These souls work within their light body, which is contained within the etheric. We urge you to concentrate on the emergence of the light body. It is composed of fine energy and has increasing purpose outside the physical. It constantly links and attunes to higher dimensional levels. Through Cosmic awareness and light, you experience the wholeness and oneness of the Universe - not in seeing or observing, but in becoming it. This in turn opens to other dimensions, involving the higher brain which is in tune with Cosmic thought patterning. This vibratory energy now encircling the earth has entered into your physical vehicle. Be assured that an evolutionary leap is one you are required to make. It will take place in many of you at this time. The future of the Earth is in your hands. We are here to assist you in love and light. May the force be with you.

Given l9th August 1993

We have in the last few channellings spoken of matters pertaining to coming world events. Now we wish to speak to you concerning Cosmic energy. Increasing light energy is pouring into your world at present. These energies are entering at points opening up within the etheric body. The etheric houses the light body which will fulfil many new functions outside the physical in the near future. One function will be to act as an absorber, collecting and retaining Cosmic rays, preventing excessive shock to the physical. The light body is made up of fine energy fibres which connect to the main Universal Grid or Source. It will serve as the main input for these new energy centres or frequencies. As you open to the entry of Cosmic rays, the light body becomes stronger, resonating and pulsating with heightened consciousness and vitality. Allowing that frequency to sound its Cosmic note causes all to reverberate within the Universal core.

Open to Cosmic light, which connects to the mental plane at present. In using the Disc frequency you are enabled to send out energy to those around you. Many souls will receive light as you transmit. There are souls in great need of your light and love. Group work will create a stronger energy field for transmission. In these new light centres all are the leaders, all working with the same ray energy. Some may only remain with you for a short time, leaving you to form other cell centres of light. All work with these new energies. You will recognise them as they come to you, many unbidden. There exists at this time a common soul identity which attracts and bonds to like soul. By contacting this frequency, healing becomes automatic. It simply takes place without effort on the part of the healer. Those who are not healed have chosen to remain where they are in the present evolutionary cycle. They are not your responsibility. All contacting these new frequencies know this to be the next evolutionary step. They have awaited this inception over many incarnations. Heightening of consciousness will affect many souls; disturbances within the physical body will occur from time to time. This is due to ongoing physical restructuring. Do not fear these changes, they are necessary. Even your earth is transmuting. As you begin to recognise your own Cosmic note, these energies will begin to feel more comfortable. The Disc we have given will help you to align. It transmits at Cosmic light levels. Its individual resonance is found in each soul, linking to each pulsating heart beat. After initial adjustment or fine tuning is complete, the disc links you to higher vibrational frequencies. You are then able to transmit at that frequency on the send-return basis we outlined in previous channellings. Your opening hearts will beat in unison with the universal heart of the Cosmos; you will automatically tune into that frequency. Then the partnership between yourself and the light beings grow. They will be strongly drawn towards you through the Disc. It is the same light ray on which they operate. Work is mainly on the mental plane at present. The final transition links physical and spiritual. Soon the electrical brain will open to receive the new frequencies. Mind, body, soul, all will fuse and ignite within the Cosmic fire. Open, open to Light and love. There is nothing else

Given 20th August 1993

Many of you have been asking: how does the Disc work? It would be difficult for you to comprehend this fully. The dots represent energy particles. The colour bands are the Cosmic spectrum. Energy is drawn from Universal sources. It has been allowed to move into your time. It carries its own Galactic harmonic or frequency.

The Disc, acting as a transmitter, feeds encoded signals into the higher part of the brain. This higher brain acts as a receiver directly decoding incoming information. Once the connection is established, messages are processed by amplification of Cosmic light sound waves These are as yet at levels far beyond the present human auditory system. They are unable to be deciphered within the physical. This incoming information is transmitted to the higher self for interpretation, making use of the sub-conscious brain which being totally unconditioned is therefore open to ongoing Cosmic transmission. Working on a computer basis, information selected is fed into neurons which act as switches to comprehensive understanding. This then passes through to conscious levels, affording maximum control together with a wide range of individual experience.

Most souls who link to Cosmic communication operate on a common ray frequency which facilitates entry into Cosmic channels. The principal aim is to assist in raising conscious awareness. The Disc, also teaching at higher self level, increases Cosmic energy. We have in previous messages taught you how the Disc may be harnessed in many different ways. Daily usage is recommended, followed by meditation. The Disc also links to the new energy points or centres forming now within the etheric. This method of communication feeds and nurtures the spiritual body with Cosmic energies which support and strengthen its new structure.

Light rays emitted from the Disc are readily absorbed by this new light body which is emerging from the etheric; both are Cosmic in origin. Light infiltration may be seen as an ongoing nurturing process for the emergence of the new body. Some of you may fail to recognise or to communicate with the Disc at this stage. It is simply because you are not on that particular frequency. You will be on other frequencies, equally satisfactory for your evolutionary journey, and all are evolving in different ways. All belong to different systems within the Galaxy. This is a time for rapid exchange of energies. The energy held within the Disc discharges Solar light. This source of light is greatly needed by Earth at present, to assist in restoring balance, wholeness and healing. You have been chosen to assist the light beings in their task. They have drawn closer to you than at any other time in evolutionary history. This is why you chose to incarnate at this critical time when the forces of darkness will make their last stand. Go forward in light and love; it is only fear which could hold you back. Go forward then as co-light workers. Love will prevail.

Given 2lst August 1993

Many of you will have worked at Third Ray levels. This Ray involves active intelligence. Predominantly it is the Ray of Love and Wisdom, manifesting in every particle of living matter, infiltrating into the spiritual nature of man. In supporting both polarities, it increases spiritual action by transformative evolvement. By promoting growth in the physical, emotional and mental bodies, all three are fused in awakening spiritual regeneration which bonds more closely to the Universal mind of which man is ongoing thought.

From your Solar Sun, seven rays emanate. These continue to pour into planetary substance, giving life and energy to all matter. Each ray has its own note, colour and vibratory level. With Cosmic energy entering earth levels at new frequencies, Ray emanations are changed. These adapt to new mutational patterns. There will be a creation of one new single ray which souls working towards completed evolutionary cycles will recognise. The input at spiritual levels advances towards Cosmic awareness and Light Source. The new Ray is composed of a single beam of pure white light and is composed of different frequencies. The knowledge of this new Ray will take strong precedence in the minds of men, being the direct light of the Logos, and therefore overtly desirable to mankind at a time when all are seeking light. The action of this Solar Light Ray will create unprecedented action upon the DNA and body cells. It will create the Light body which emerges from the heavy vehicle of matter. The Light body is the evolutionary leap forward. It becomes a door to higher dimensional states. Many will enter by this door, others will re-incarnate to other planetary systems for ongoing soul-development.

It is true to state, nothing will ever be the same. As you open to this spiritual nature, the light body will then open to new dimensions. Discernment will be razor-sharp; the thoughts and minds of others will be disclosed to you with amazing clarity. This surge of pure energy will raise you to wholeness and Cosmic light which is total knowing, total discernment, total being. This is not a psychic awakening, but rather Cosmic in origin. In this state, intuition alone will dictate the need to help or to leave alone. Many will not stand with you; they will walk away in fear and without understanding. They are not your responsibility. Some will attack you because they will be unable to tolerate your growing light. Fear closes to the Christ Light. You will be given the ability now to see clearly whatever is not of the Light. Understand that changes are registering most acutely now, within the emotional body. There will be massive clearing of past conditioning. You will effectively clear this accumulated debris. The healing of past memories is something taking place in many souls, it is needed to create new space for new spiritual energies. Remember your spiritual nature is strongly attracted now to the Christ Light. The seed has been sown. Its flowering hour lies within the heart of pure Cosmic light. The magnetism of this pure light will pull you upwards into its pathway. This is your Spiritual destiny. Love and light.

Given 23rd August 1993

The structure of the disc is suspended in vibrational energy. This structure exists in all physical systems. Everything within the Universe is in constant motion. This is due to the invisible vibration of light waves. In this perpetual movement, atoms and molecules emit and absorb electromagnetic energy. All is energy, all is vibrational. In altered states of consciousness, which the Disc may at times promote, there are structural changes to matter and energy. Physical concepts of reality may be re-energised or accelerated. Structure may change as light waves convert or connect to alternative systems which perceive new boundaries of time and space. This may produce experience of parallel worlds or different systems in time and space. These altered states, or out of the body experiences, take place in the higher brain or nervous system.

Tuning into higher energies promotes discernment into orderly or disorderly vibrational patterns within the physical emotional and mental bodies of man. Cosmic healing is based upon seeing disorderly photons (or rhythms) within, and working to create new viable or stable states of re-connected energy patterns. Such healing is achieved through visualisation and sound frequencies. Using the inner mind to view images of healthy or distorted energy patterns which are either disruptive or beneficial to connective organs and nervous systems, diagnosis is obtained. This new method is not linked to existing treatment programmes. It is a new way of learning to heal, working with those areas of the brain which are opening to the higher vibrational energies which also create experience of parallel worlds or altered states.

This new way of working with frequencies or vibratory levels, implies opening your minds in faith and trust and moving away from old conditioning which has served until now as building blocks for the majority of healers. As the mind opens, you will perceive clearly body imbalance. Your ears, attuning to disrupted resonance flowing from the affected area, pick up depleted vibrational frequency. Such blocked areas are unable to permit healthy energy flow from other connected organs, and consequently become clogged, impaired and isolated within the total system. Discordant levels will, with continued practice, register acutely in your minds. The new light body will also register areas which are out of balance. Dysfunction cuts off from other resonating healthy cellular structures. This leads to breakdown of the system and in some cases permits no return to original cell reproduction.

Sound links to resonance, creating the Universal note. When the harmonic is contacted. there is always orderly return or re-issue to diseased matter or fluctuating levels of energy. A return to Universal laws is effected. The Disc resonates at inaudible sound levels, activating healing energies. This may be seen as pulsating or moving. This vibrational energy in motion may be harnessed for the new healing.

Given 25th August 1993

As an increase in light enters the Earth, the greater the absorption of darkness. The latter is eliminated by vibrating waves of light. These act upon higher frequencies to subdue, bringing density into control. The incoming light prevents future unattached accumulations of darkness drifting on or about the Earth. The strengthening rays of the Cosmic Sun will gradually increase the luminosity of Earth Ultimately as darkness disperses, its particles will spin out into space void. As Light increases in clarity, its volume will finally envelop Earth's total surface. Day and night will be indistinguishable. The sun providing strong insulation will radiate increased heat, giving rise to such planetary brightness, as to be seen clearly by Star systems within different galaxies. These changes will take place gradually. The Earth will gain a second sun, already forming, soon to emerge as the Principal, our own sun becoming its satellite. This will bring about stronger ray emanations. Both suns will regulate the ongoing influx of light. Ultra violet Rays will enter more directly into the Earth's atmosphere. These rays entering now are not powerful enough to cause any ill effect. As man's immune system is restructured, an increase in ray power will occur. The light body will be able to deflect all negative energies emanating from Gamma and Ultra Violet light, previously held to be dangerous to cell structure. The light body possesses the ability to deflect such Ray input. Earth dweller's vision has been evolutionary darkened until now. This has enabled light to be received at lower accommodating levels, and has included his present mode of interpreting light and darkness. When his eyes open to Cosmic light, his present mode of seeing will be restructured. He will see without damage to optic nerve or retina. This alignment is taking place in many of you at present. Some discomfort may occur from time to time, disorientation or headache. It is a temporary state. Appropriate alignment will protect you from Rays which when entering the physical, would cause malignant cell change. The light body when completely developed will enable you to resort to its new structure in complete safety. This is one of the main reasons for its creation. It will sustain frequencies of Ultra Violet and Gamma Rays without incurring metabolic change.

The present atmosphere of the Earth will gradually change. due to the closer proximity of two suns. It will become gaseous, highly charged, and prohibitive to life as you presently experience it. Even by averting cataclysmic disasters within the next ten years, even by avoidance of major catastrophic events, this evolutionary change or shift will take place. Future man by then may have prepared himself by scientific advancement, to journey into other worlds, since this planet will become increasingly unstable, and consequently unable to support life in its present form. Such is the cycle of evolution. Your world will ascend, orbit and ultimately become a bright star in space. The death of one world, brings forth another, giving existence to new life forms which are yet other expressions of the Creative love which birthing all life, finally gathers them back to the

Source. We stand in planetary time and space. Past, present and future, all is now .We sound the timeless note of Cosmic Creation.

<u>Given 26th August 1993</u>

Your present understanding of light is measured against the opposite polarity of darkness: the separation of light and dark particles. Young, undeveloped souls are strongly influenced by darkness. They are drawn towards it. It is seen in your time strongly representative of primitive ego strengths demanding instant self gratification. The evolving soul's understanding of light is reflected in his desire to attract it always towards him. It is seen as the predominating note of individual spiritual ascension. Here gratification is delayed, strengthened by the Super-Ego (higher self).

Darkness and light cannot exist together. One supplants the other. Darkness is composed of opaque vibratory energy. It has a dense molecular structure which renders it impervious to light. The new energy waves of Cosmic light entering into Earth now are God-Light. This light absorbs and restructures particles of negativity (dark energy), transforming them into light waves with faster frequencies. The light frequencies combine to eliminate all former dense structure.

Until now darkness has competed with light. It has mimicked procreative acts, generating seeds, human birth (the womb) etc. Such creative patterns incur the natural law of decay and death. Had germination processed in total light, the DNA would have not carried these penalties. Darkness crept across the face of the Earth at the Dawn of time, linking to man's separation from the Source (Light). In your world, death is accepted as inevitable. As darkness is now gradually brought under control, it will be absorbed, eliminated and finally replaced by the radiance of light. As it weakens, planetary healing will ensue.

Ongoing creation of the Light Body implies that there can be no retention of darkness within its structure. As it is constantly absorbing light rays, and is nurtured by light, there is total resistance to dark energy. Subject to the natural laws of light, the Light Body pertains specifically to the Crown of Light, which is the Logos or Source. Therefore it is not subject to either decay or death. It is an integral part of man's spiritual nature, a soul-component, and therefore immortal. On the death of the physical, it detaches itself, forming eternal union with the Source from whom it has never at any time separated. It has always been in existence. At this time it is to integrate strongly into the physical, forming a spiritual base within the etheric. It is seen as ongoing evolutionary spiritual development, creating as it will a new dimension for man.

Everything taking place at the present time has always been an essential part of the plan. You are participators by free choice. Light is pouring out in abundance now, darkness will be forced back. It will flee because the Light is stronger, ultimately dispersing. Your planet will become again a world of radiant love and light. You will then inhabit a new garden of Eden as spiritual beings, walking in the light of the Cosmic Sun.

Given 29th August 1993

Aligning with Universal Cosmic Forces implies entering into harmony with the energies of the Earth itself. Think, breathe, and connect to the Cosmic note which is the expression of Universal Love. Many of you are beginning to realise that there are many selves. All are inter-related and connected to this Universal energy which exists outside the physical body. Energy forms, brought about by creative thought into matter and being, remain permanently connected to the Source. You share kinship with all nature. All are joined as one, in the same vibrating energy. Your conditioning has served to prohibit creativity and awareness. This was originally perceived with inner eyes and ears. These have grown into disuse due to centuries of false ego perception which has dulled the eye of spirit. You and all beings form part of a complex whole which touches in and out of energy levels, ceaselessly and repetitively, interchanging every moment you breathe. This vital force is taken in through the electric body, and transmitted to physical, emotional and mental bodies through the wheels of energy control centres. You would be unable to exist in your present life form, operating at physical body levels, alone. This body is dependent upon other subtle energy bodies for continued well-being. If the energy flow is obstructed in any of them, then all becomes unbalanced and affected. This imbalance is felt mainly at the physical level.

You know so little about your own spiritual nature, and so much about inconsequential affairs. Take time to centre yourselves. Go within more frequently to communicate powerfully with that which is outside. As you practise, mainly by breathing in vital energy, conscious levels will expand and you will grow in insight, accessing to non physical realms and worlds. Your present perception will change, reality transmuting into its true nature of spiritual energy. Remember, all energy is a force of vital power which the subconscious mind clothes in thought. Words are the outcome of energised thought at Conscious mind levels. The higher self uses images or symbols, involving a different part of the brain for interpretation. The energy you transmit affects all within the total network. You will begin to be aware of emerging powers, inherent in the new light body, so the energy transmitted will be of a finer quality. This energy will be used to heal, protect and sustain you in days to come. Be aware then of the power of your thoughts and the energy which clothes them. Grow in spiritual awareness and increase in soul-strengths. In time you will realise the potential to project your mind from the body. In these altered states, the brightest star in the heavens may be seen.

This is part of the Ancient Wisdom originally brought to earth from outer space at the dawn of time. Man possessed the ability then to enter into such inter-dimensional states. Conditioning had no conscious hold upon him. Gradually, as man became increasingly materialistic, this gift was lost to Earth. It is only now brought back once more, in trust and love. The dubious of this world will plead the impossibility of such knowledge, and against the backdrop of centuries of Ego-conditioning.

Crop circles, which are strongly in evidence today, may indicate old power spots which were originally connected to the Earth's harmonic note or frequency. This early matrix of Cosmic energy was integrated into the Earth's structure at the time of its formation, serving as a constantly returning and emerging power line to main Galactic grids. Early man knew the sacredness of such sites and drew Cosmic power from them, acting as an intermediary between Earth and the Galaxy. The earth was re-charged and revitalised by the interchange of these energies, its balance maintained by the constant flow. As man moved away from his original priestly role, the Ancient Wisdom was also lost. Today it may yet be seen in all its primordial splendour, existing among primitive tribes who have retained it by their continued closeness with Nature and their strong beliefs in the mystical power of the Cosmic Universe.

In western cultures, Cosmic power spots have lain submerged under dense blanketing of negative dark energy for millions of earth years. Now the breath of the Cosmic wind with its strong light emission clears away debris; it enables a surfacing or rising effect of the original power grid which, upon reshaping, appears once more on the Earth's surface. This indicates a return of the Ancient Wisdom. As Earth is now in the final act of effecting rebalance, there is also a corresponding shift to original line and symmetry. The residual energy emanating from such power sites has always remained within the earth and now, when Cosmic energy is re-entering Earth at faster changed levels, the restructuring of former cosmically designed power grids or lines becomes evident. As the original structure was never changed, only hidden until man was empowered to recognise it, it may now emerge as a pertinent tool for the future dwellers of this planet.

Given 30th August 1993

For those of you who feel that contact healing is important, we would say, if you cannot accept that vibrational energy transfer is possible without the use of hands, then you must come to our way of healing as and when you are able to do so. This implies opening your minds, allowing the new methods of healing to imprint at acceptable levels. What you have been registering with your hands is information concerning the imbalance of vibrational energy, in physical organs and cells. All your sensory measuring devices have been involved in this process. Information being fed into the mind, you have completed your diagnosis. Energy is then transferred by the mind to the hands.

When you heal directly with the mind, an energy transfer takes place. The only difference being that physical touch is not employed. When you touch physically you are imprinting into another's energy circuits, often emotionally, although not intentionally. Healing by thought directs finer energy, increasing diagnostic skills. Using the mental body protects against unconscious intrusion into a patient's vibratory level. To assess and heal mentally gives the healing process over to the higher or intuitive mind. This is called telepathy healing and is linked to new Cosmic energies which harness man's own resonating energy field in the healing dialogue.

When you heal by direct physical contact, you must be aware that you are also transmitting your own resonance and vibratory level to others. If your own energy is low or blocked in any way, if imbalance in any particular organ or cell exists, there is an immediate transfusion or transfer from healer to receiver of this imbalance. You may deplete your recipient, taking more than you offer. This is of course operates at levels outside your conscious mind. Those of you who are Sensitives are open to receiving conditions which may be transferred to you in this way. Even assuming careful protection is inherent in the healing programme, this can and does take place. Maximum protection is to be found in non-contact healing methods.

Opening your minds to New Healing techniques implies moving away from past learnt responses regarding healing methods generally. Those of you on the new frequency or wave form will accept in totality these channellings, since they will appear recognisable at higher self level. You have all worked in this way in past lives. It is acceptable to extend the hands and arms towards the person you are healing: this conveys love, an expression which the recipient may appreciate. In time, however, you will learn to express love with your mind only. If you will remember methods of Absent Healing, which many of you practise, this is not so very different. Physically you are absent, your patient at a distance.

You send out healing with mind thought, directing light and love in healing energy waves. They do of course reach the person they are intended for, since all thought is energy in motion. This form of healing is powerfully transmitted. This non-conditional healing involves mind projected energy, employing the same principles as Cosmic healing. Peace and healing to you all.

Given 2nd September 1993

Your survival will depend upon your individual response, and the ongoing development of the light body. This body will be able to convert light into usable energy. It possesses the ability to deflect harmful rays and, being heat resistant, it is impervious to high temperatures. The fine energy fibres of light will enclose the physical body against any intrusion of rays which could alter normal cell function. Compared to a space suit which is totally impenetrable, it will afford maximum protection to its wearer. In time to come the Light body will appear, emanating from the etheric, seen by the naked eye as a vaporous misty light surrounding existing body structure. The emergence of this body may now be seen by those of you who are Sensitives. Some of you have confused it with the Aura. It is entirely independent.

Due to evolutionary and mutational change, food will have a different input and output. As the immune system develops, new organic structure will change your present use of food. What you eat in future will consist of a different cellular structure. Energy, in its purest form of light, may be part of this intake. The head and brain area are to receive maximum protection, insulated by regulating frequencies which are able to increase insulation, if required. Climatic changes will necessitate this. The light body will draw in rays of continuous energy, re-charging itself from Cosmic light. When this occurs, the existing volume of body density will diminish. This will give rise to lightness of body, enabling you to move at increased speed and height. Some of you may have experienced this in out of the body states. Those of you who will choose, or who have already chosen, to remain, assisting the Earth Guardians, will be required to undergo this mutational change. Widespread chaotic and changeable climatic conditions will occur. This will be due to the Earth's efforts to effect rebalance, or to re-orbit in a new path. Where such situations occur, you may be in imminent danger, then the light body will afford fast exit. Acting upon a Hyper-Wave system, light energy will enter an orbiting state to protect and remove you to a safe area.

Land beings will in time evolve into Air beings. This mutational transition is requisite. The lower atmosphere of the Earth will in time become increasingly unstable, and consequently unsafe for ongoing gravitational pull. It would be impossible for you to continue in your present form. Do not be fearful of these changes; they will be gradual and take place over a period of time. For those of you who lack courage to contemplate this, other forms of existence will be offered to you, on many different planes within the Universe. For the young and undeveloped soul, opportunity for continuation of the Karmic contract will be given. For those souls able to understand and accept our channellings, we say to you, your Karma has now passed. It is completed. However, no soul will be lost. Ultimately, all will stand within their final dimension of pure light. It is Universal Cosmic Law. If you have chosen this path, know there can be no return. You will remain to assist the Guardians of Earth. This was always your spiritual destiny: to serve humanity in its hour of need.

     <u>Given 5th September 1993</u>

Intergalactic communication is composed of varying signals, each overlapping into the frequencies of different planets. By harnessing these signals we are able to gain information regarding global function or dysfunction. The main energy input for these signals is the Universal Cosmic grid. We maintain and monitor this grid which is in constant movement, and whose ceaseless energy flow emanates from the Logos or Source.

     We have monitored the progress of Earth over many years. It saddens us to see the reckless defiance of man, who continues to destroy its natural resources. We tell you that, if this state continues, man will succeed in the total annihilation of himself and all living things. Your planet, men of earth, cannot survive in an increasingly unstable orbit. This unpredictability will increase, affecting everyone within the near future, unless there is radical change.

     If intergalactic communication is to take place in the foreseeable future, it will teach moral and ethical values which may bring your world into line with other worlds far in advance of your own Solar system. Until you reach certain levels, the natural Cosmic law will preclude such an event taking place. This implies, at present, enforced isolation regarding contact with other Solar systems in proximity to your own. There is of course ongoing surveillance and scrutiny by the Earth Guardians, who have drawn closer to you in these days of dire need. We, together with them, are transmitting to those of you who are open and will listen to our words. We are sustaining you with hope for your dying world. Our main work is to enable you to expand in consciousness, thereby raising vibratory levels. If this course of action is effected, you may be able to sustain a predictable and stable future for your Planet.

     There exists a global system of control for all life. This universal control is attempting to re-stabilise and maintain an even orbiting path for Earth, even now. This may only be realised if a growing sense of overall responsibility for the world in which you live ensues. You will have to move away from present attitudes which are contributing to imbalance. You are breaking the Natural laws of the Universe. Man will only bring about ultimate destruction as long as he remains in a state of constant flux and disharmony within himself, failing to contact his real spiritual nature.

Our present attempt to communicate with you carries the approval of the Earth Guardians. By raising present levels of planetary consciousness, your future could stabilise. We speak within you always. Many will hear and their lives will change. The mind is the instrument for such change. Spiritual revolution may save your planet from its downward spiral and consequent disaster. Charge up your vibrational energies, directing light and love towards Earth. Each one is a Healer with a vast reservoir of Cosmic energy. We are helping you to transmit light as a healing force. Your individual ascension is tied to that of Earth; you are now in process of returning to the Source as pure light beings. This is your spiritual destiny.

Given 7th September 1993

With the new energies entering the earth at the present time, we feel it important to give you information concerning fifth dimensional experience. Within you there is a "silent" area of the brain. This silent area is untouched by the middle brain with its functioning of inrushing thought and ego conditioned projecting. Here is the essence of the true self or being. In meditation this centre is activated into expansive consciousness. This cellular component is an evolutionary transplant, a spiritual umbilical cord connecting you to the Logos or Source. Activating this area directs you towards higher states of consciousness. As you draw closer to the light, you will experience the vibratory quality of this new energy. The physical body will feel transfused, irradiated. Every molecule, every cell flooded with Cosmic power and energy. You will become the light as it pours through you. This spiritual tidal wave carries you into fifth dimensional time and space. Its tremendous power is pure flame energy. In such states, lightness of body is often experienced. As movement is at a different frequency, it does not require the normal physical input. Because there has been experience of an altered state there will also be communication. You will be entering these states with increased frequency as light enters into you. This entry into the light body is life, not death. This is the individual ascension.

The new energies will help you to effect this transition with ease. There will be no excessive jolting to the nervous system, which will remain as "watchdog" in the process, returning you to third dimensional levels if there is any unprotected exposure which could prove dangerous to present existence. Ultimately both hemispheres of the brain will balance to assimilate this higher self information, and this will formulate to a sense of well being together with increased vitality and power. The energy taken in by you will be purer, finer, and so will be absorbed quickly. The awakened sleeping centres will be stimulated to higher expansiveness of consciousness. With this higher evolutionary state, there will also be a growing desire to become more spiritually aware and to realise union with the Source. This state of enlightenment will be recognised ultimately at conscious levels.

A portal is now opening to many of you who are evolving. You have awaited this development over many earth life incarnations. All are in the process of returning to Source. Everything within you is awakening now. There will be a sharp increase in clarity and perception, together with the growing recognition of your real place within the Cosmic order. Heightened sensitivity will enable you to see with new vision the unfolding living Universe, and the knowledge of your true spiritual nature. Previously this state of enlightenment was granted to a few chosen souls, and only after lifetimes of seeking and austerity. These ascended masters have left their own residual energy which still serves to replenish the earth. You are going forward into this new evolutionary cycle. As you are drawn towards the light, you will become that light. When you are total light beings, then fifth dimensional time is entered.

Given 10th September 1993

There is at present an ongoing emptying out process taking place in souls. It could be compared to a sort of house move, where priority has to be given as to what is to be discarded, and what is to be saved. In such events, much rubbish has accumulated and a lot of it must be thrown away as many items are no longer required. You are in a similar situation. You too are moving towards a new structure, a new being. The old inherited pattern of genetic DNA and its counterpart, which have remained encoded within you, is being renewed or altered to mutable change. Ongoing mutability restructures the cellular structure of the genes, breaking away from old repetitive patterning. Such changes occur at new evolutionary cycles. This implies new patterns of learning and different responses in changing situations. Inherent conditioning is also involved in this new restructuring.

The existing DNA structure is to be changed. Extra chromosomes will form in addition to the present double helix. Within your existing bodies cellular change takes place every few years - hair, skin cell renewal etc. You are totally unaware of these changes; nevertheless they take place. With the coming of the new evolutionary cycle, many changes will occur. Your new cellular structure will give you different abilities.

Before this can take place, there needs to be a cleansing, an emptying out. Not only of the genetic structure, but also of past behavioural patterns which have sprung from past inherited conditioning responses. As these clear, the new spiritual being emerges. This change will ensue from the creation and implant of a single new cell. This cell will propagate new cells to identical form and structure, the old cell genetic coding gradually being replaced by the latter. The interchange will be viable throughout, causing little body dysfunction during the replacement process. Monitored symbiotic symmetry will protect against double functioning levels as new and old overlap during the initial period.

There will also be organic changes to the brain. This will occur as a gradual process, causing minimal disturbance, during the transitional period. Noticeably the changes will take place within the mid-brain, which acts impulsively and often emotionally. Preference will be given to the Cortex with its slower calculative cycle. Finally the cerebellum will enlarge. This part of the brain will act quickly to assimilate new patterns of restructured thought and energy, accepting ongoing change with logical reasoning as being an integral part of the new natural order. The new species will be light of body, able to respond more effectively to climatic change.

Remember your early origins and recall how man was required to adjust to mutational change. Your present body bears little resemblance to that of your primitive ancestors. As the earth changed, man adjusted in order to survive. Now you are facing the greatest change for thousands of years. It is entirely due to imminent change within your Solar system. If you are to survive, then new mutational patterns are seen as requisite. This is not a retrograde step, rather an evolutionary leap forward into a new dimension.

Given llth September 1993

Consciousness is growing and expanding within you. We see this growth as the unfolding petals of a beautiful flower. The seed of Cosmic light has been implanted in your souls. Now it unfolds, attracting light towards it. The heart of this flower is a reflection of the Cosmos itself. It holds the rainbowed light of the Cosmic spectrum, and within its final flowering hour lie seeds of spiritual fruition. These will be scattered to the four corners of the Earth. Wherever they seed themselves, total transformation will take place within a blaze of Cosmic colour and light. This light is the Cosmic fire which, when absorbed into your etheric, burns away the base metal of dark energy exposing the true colour and vibrancy of soul-light.

The flame of this fire is both purifying and cleansing, burning without heat or fierceness. Promoting the flow of Cosmic Light Space, it opens the heart portals to new Dimensional experience. Penetrating bone, blood and cellular structure, its ongoing infusion creates the new Cosmic being who stands in total balance, within both hemispheres of heaven and earth, his body admitting no boundaries of time or space. He is at once the Cosmic whole, his outstretched arms encompassing humanity in an endless cycle of unconditional love and light.

Being enlightened, man now sees all things as an integral part of an ongoing whole, ceaselessly and endlessly joined in a cycle of dimensional time which is now. His eyes being opened to his own spiritual dimension, he is able to enter this gateway as true heir and co-creator. With the breath of the Cosmic wind enkindling his spirit, he becomes open to fifth Dimensional incoming thought and experience. The new vibrational energies seek out his highest frequency or connective point to infuse and transmit Universal light and knowledge. In this enlightened state, he stands as an intermediary between Earth and the Universe. As everything is drawn into and through his own soul energy, there is the ultimate realisation and understanding of his own Christ role and meaning. He then becomes his own Christ light entering symbolically as the ageless Cosmic Christ.

We who are of the Light and who have always stood within the Light marvel at this metamorphosis of man finally emerging from the gross body into his true spiritual dimension. You are all in the process of becoming the Light. As you absorb it, there will be an experience of ensuing lightness within the physical vehicle. Know that darkness is presently being overcome by light. It is in the process of dispersing or fleeing Earth. As this takes place, there will be great resistance on the part of unspiritual man to block this process. Although it might appear to many souls that this dark energy pattern will ultimately emerge as the victor, we tell you that in the final outcome light will triumphantly prevail.

Given 13th September 1993

The light body is a luminous field of light surrounding the human form. It is triggered by electromagnetic energy which, moving faster than the speed of light, links to different channels or frequencies. When such frequencies are received, the electric component of the light body, becoming activated, serves as a sensitive sensor to assimilate incoming signals, decoding them. The luminous activity of soul energy is reflected in the extending emanations of this body. These are emerging now in increased and projected states. As soul-light is absorbed, it both strengthens and feeds the Light body for future functioning, constantly patterning and re-aligning to Cosmic rays which overlap and penetrate by wave form. Its cycle is orbicular, forming structured repetitive resonating energy. Seen outside the physical body by those of you who are sensitives, it will present as radiating spirals of multicoloured light. In time its resonance will infiltrate the physical, creating subtle and vibrant interaction. When this is implemented, both physical and etheric will merge and unite.

In the future this energy will be visible to all. It will serve as an ongoing indication of awakened spiritual man. Many souls will shine with this light. They will be recognised as shining beacons in the period when no light is entering Earth. This spiritual substance is composed of luminosity which glows in darkness. Souls attuned to Cosmic frequencies will attract spectrumed light particles which will strongly attach to the Light body. Light extent will reflect depth of Ray saturation transferred to the Etheric body, emanating from The Cosmic Sun which is openly revealed to the initiated.

These souls will develop an inbuilt radar, receiving and transmitting Cosmic frequencies, piloting souls to a safe haven in times of distress. Many will call to them and be heard, for the Cosmic heart rests in a state of open and unconditional love. Such hearts have been empowered to serve in days of darkness and great need. These are the co-guardians of Earth in the latter days. When the Cosmic note is heard vibrant levels of sound and colour, unprecedented in worlds of time and space, will occur. The Cosmic note joins all energies together in muted vibrancy, in wordless synchronization. This note will be relayed to listening stations around the Universal Galaxy. The joining of powerful resonating energies will create endless Cosmic overspill into Earth space. When this takes place all souls will awaken to transcend. Then the physical being taken up will ultimately merge and attune to the Light body which is eternal. This is future man in spiritual guise.

You are now in preparation for the coming time when the portent sign will be visible, significantly displayed as a new bright roseate star, prominent within the heavens, and suspended between two other stars of lesser hue. This Star will be large, appearing to be closer to earth than those now immediately visible. There will be a close proximity to a great white light, which is the Solar Sun. When these are seen, know that it is a clear sign and symbolic manifestation of the last cycle.

Given 15th September 1993

What awareness do you have regarding your spiritual identity? You know many other factors concerning yourself, accumulating such data over many life years. You are a Cosmic being with a spiritual centre. The Centre contains your point of being and connectedness with the network of all other spiritual essences and energies. It is this part alone which is immortal, returning to the Logos who created you from its first breath. You have existed in Cosmic worlds long before incarnation into your present physical body, the latter acting as a temporary abode or structure for soul experience upon the Earth plane. As soon as you were clothed in flesh, you began to return, to ascend, your consciousness unfolding with soul development. It was your choice to come to earth, to experience birth, life and death in mortal perishable guise. During this time your eyes have been closed to the Light and vision of the Cosmos. In your sleep, and in out of the body states, you have returned to that Divine light many times to be replenished and irradiated by it. Within that original point of being, your spiritual identity was always manifest. These spiritual returns have until now been at a sub-conscious level in states of altered consciousness when you have experienced union with the Source. Such merging or melding transforms all souls with the pure flame of Cosmic awareness. In these states the soul is elevated towards blissful unknowing. Divine consciousness is realised. All are then caught up in a single act of becoming, all being held in a timeless moment of now.

The Cosmic Disc is a minute reflection of this pure energy. Its light is vibrational energy. As you receive its transmissions, you become spiritually enlightened. You are given only as much as the physical can hold in protective love and wisdom. As you receive its resonance, your true spiritual identity is experienced. At such moments the desire to return to the Source, the connective point of being, will register strongly as you are drawn towards the centre of Universal Love. This pervasive love is everywhere, entering into your own spiritual centre, and opening the Portal door to Cosmic heavens.

At this point in time, an increase in expanding consciousness will reveal your true spiritual identity. Breathed out by The Logos, you were always a child of the Universe, an immortal and spiritual soul. Now more than ever your eyes are opening to the light of the Cosmic Galaxy. In time, and as consciousness unfolds, you will cross Cosmic space faster than the speed of light and sound, within the protection of the new light body. All this was part of the original contract, ultimately transcending to the total realisation of your true spiritual dimension. Man came from beyond the stars into earth existence and experience. Now as he in the act of completing this evolutionary cycle, he is enabled to return to his original point of uncreated being, resting agelessly within the essence and heartbeat of the Cosmos of which he was always an integral part, to which he was always united and joined. We are therefore your true brothers and work towards your reunion and joyful return. With an increase in love and light.

Given 17th September 1993

Your expanding consciousness now enables you to trigger higher vibrational energy through the molecular structure. Once oscillation occurs, rapid acceleration of neuron activity ensues. Your energy converters now carry elevated states of positive love and joy which are flowing through widened and sensitised centres of communication. The space station of your subconscious mind is our point of entry or connectedness. Listen to the colours we make in you. Our form is light and colour imbued. Our reflection is held in brightness and sunlight. In the rainbowed spectrum of the cosmic disc, you may see us. We are the centre, point of being, or concentricity.

Your own resonance becomes our input for light energy. The higher the resonating flow, the greater the absorption of light particles. Increased vibratory flow creates a field of accelerated modulation. Breathe in light, and as you breathe it out it will spiral to create repetitive cycles of energy. Your mind is attuning to your own Cosmic note. This note reverberates at resonating levels extending beyond the etheric. In time you will hear, feel or see not only your own Cosmic pulse but also the Cosmic frequencies of others. By tuning into levels which when experienced present as either flowing or depleted, you will recognise that altered resonance indicates dysfunction at physical, mental or emotional levels, giving rise to imbalance within the total energy system. The gift of discernment will enable you to re-correct imbalance with a surcharge of healing energy directed out in light rays. This implies overall responsibility together with an appropriate healing dialogue between healer and patient. Never impose your own resonance upon another without their consent. Failure to secure such could drain the healer of vital energy reserves, reversing the healing process.

As you draw towards the light and breathe it in, souls will be drawn towards you because there is recognition of that vibrancy. This energy will resonate and blend with individual frequencies, creating further opening of the heart area and finally triggering synchronous sound and colour. Love will be magnified so that all will seek this quality in others, uniting to create a fire which is inextinguishable. The heart energy will elevate all souls to move towards Cosmic awareness.

This is the force awakening within you, and as you experience its powerful workings, then all minds will open fully to the Cosmic Vision. All things being perceived within this light become one. Everything is seen as connected to the Source and emanating from therein. You are now empowered to realise your spiritual stature which is great. Direct purposeful thought energy towards the Earth which will readily absorb your light. We require your spiritual input to dispel large areas of density which prevent light flow. These areas are depleted in energy, their resonance blanketed by heavy inert matter which is only dispersed by light infiltration. You are the new light carriers, choosing to incarnate on earth at this time, emerging as healers of the Planet. We shall assist you to heal your Earth in love and light. By so doing you will discharge your spiritual contract made in love many incarnations ago.

Given 20th September 1993

Cosmic inhalation implies inbreathing of resonating energy through picture absorption. As the colours increases in vibrancy, an increase in spiritual energy takes place. This is always at individual level. Instead of the usual visual intake, there is also use of the sensory areas. This includes smell and taste. The soul or spiritual essence of the picture is taken in by the nose and mouth. This releases the scent or elixir, which when strongly experienced, results in elevating electromagnetic fields. As it merges and diffuses within the cellular structure, it contacts the higher brain, there exciting neurons to distribute its informative process to brain cells and promoting altered states of consciousness. It is then exhaled on the out breath to perfume widely, contacting other souls within its frequency range and amplifying a thousandfold. The circular structure or boundary of all Cosmic pictures symbolically represents Universal dimensions. The colour coded particles are open ended energy portals which are ceaselessly making spiralling contact with all existing matter. It is the Cosmic heart which is especially open to the coloured sound which emanates from the pulsating centre. The rhythmical vibration emitted by the pictures expands and contracts at a rate similar to your own heart beat or pulse, becoming melded and united with the latter. Daily use of Cosmic picture energy increases the frequency of transmissions, especially when used in conjunction with the channelling. Transmission activates soul-energy and produces orientated thought-energy sequences. When this occurs, there is simultaneous bonding between the two hemispheres of heaven and earth.

Practised repetitive visualization leads to an eventual mind image formation without physical sighting of the picture. This is due to higher mind bonding. Pictures appearing at unprecedented times are recognisable by structure boundaries but may have different colour saturation. This is to match individual needs or frequencies. Discharged picture energy is always at controlled levels, meeting input throughout. Should overloading occur, there will be automatic "shut down." During early usage, there may be increased change in the hypnogogic state. Increased visual imagery implies expanding consciousness and greater opening of the subconscious mind.

We should make reference here of the second Cosmic Disc which we have brought into third dimensional time. This acts as a scanner seeking out systemic imbalance or fluctuational change. Having gauged the present metabolic rate, it then acts to restore former interrupted balance, and by creating healthier flow diffuses or penetrates blockages, presenting within the body as heavy inert energy. Disruption or ongoing blockages to energy flow lead to many unrelated illnesses or organic disease. This healing Disc stands in your time as a working tool. It has chosen to serve mankind. At all times treat the Disc with spiritual awareness. Abuse could result in an automatic "shut down"

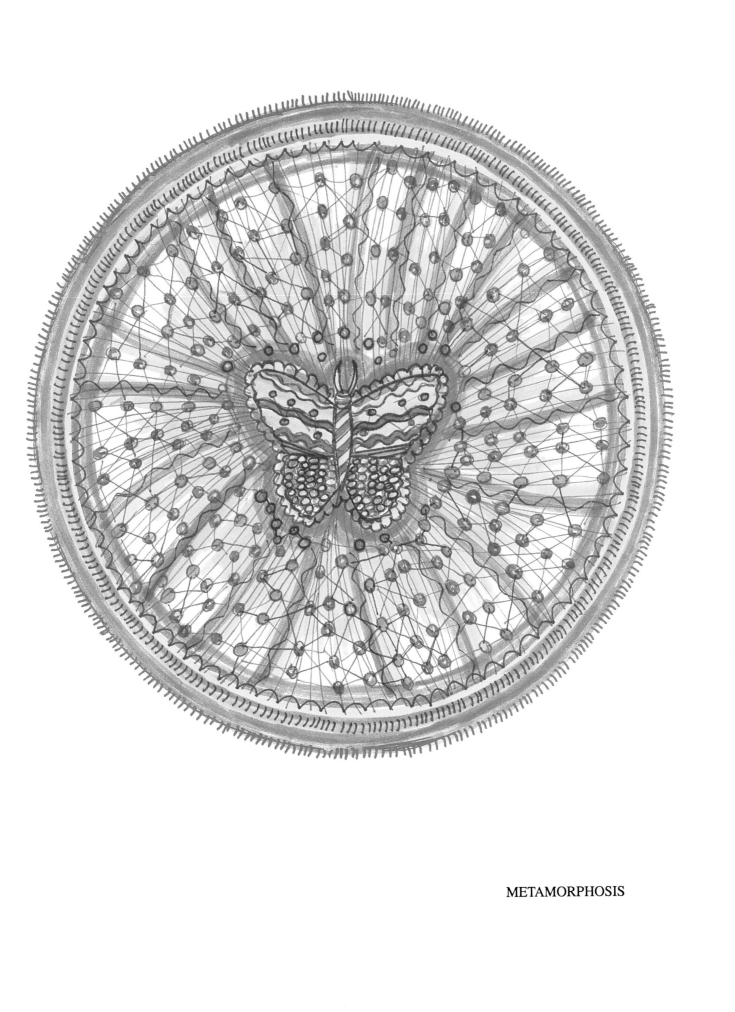

METAMORPHOSIS

which we spoke of. It is in itself a living healing entity. General reference to healing practice is set out in previous channellings. We send you always love and light.

Given 22nd September 1993

In the wake of major disasters affecting earth in which massive climatic change has taken place, there follows the inevitable aftermath of widespread epidemic disease. This is due to pollution of vital life supplies, water food, air etc. These becoming grossly contaminated or changed, give rise to numerous kinds of virus, simple organisms, smaller than bacteria, which are potential sources of widespread disease. In contained disasters affecting only a part of the earth, there is immediate emergency help, together with the aid of neighbouring countries, able to supply antidotes or medicine to counteract poisonous toxins, thereby saving life. Such affected areas are brought under control by the advances of your modern medicine and technology. In the event of any future world wide catastrophe such help would not be available, due to every part of the earth being affected at the same time.

Natural immunising agents require time in which to give long term protection against bacterial or virus invasion. Such processes take many years in which to build up in the body before the formation of effective anti-bodies. This together with common knowledge that a world wide disaster would lead to a severe scarcity of drugs or antibiotics. Viruses have always given rise to epidemics in the past million years or more, creating mutational change, or decimating an entire species. The future contains little certainty that history will not repeat itself. Such a holocaust could wipe out millions of earth creatures, totally changing earth forms as they exist at present.

To protect you against this and to offer you complete immunity, we have spoken to you concerning the future light body of man. This body is composed of spiritual energy. It is developing in many souls at present. There is rapid acceleration due now to planetary changes. Given the future event of worldwide disaster, gross pollution will give rise to major epidemics, not previously witnesses and on an unprecedented scale. Gross alteration to all life forms would follow. Changed or new bacterial strains would attack the immune system, and, in the absence of effective anti-bodies, wipe out millions. The survivors of this holocaust will result in a species who have developed immunity against bacterial invasion. These are those spiritual beings who are transferred to the light body. Because of the transparency of this body it will be possible to alter the total molecular structure to a new frequency, thus occupying different parts of space and time which are immune to disease and death.

This event may be regarded by many of you as impossible even to contemplate! May we remind you that the accomplishment of man landing upon the moon would have been seen as pure fantasy only a few years ago! Man is advancing towards the frontiers of space. As a star being he is in the act of returning. Many without total protection of the light body will not survive the journey, Preparation now is essential. Cleanse and purify the body to allow structural changes to take place This implies great trust and love. We give you this information in great love and light. We recognise your true dimensional form. Galactic brotherhood.

Given 23rd September 1993

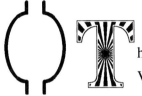 his is a Cosmic symbol and may be used in a healing programme. Visualize the person with whom you are working. Place them mentally within the boundary structure of the picture, taking care to centre them so that energy input may be balanced. The open ends of the symbol at the highest point represent a free flow of vibratory energy which is activated by mind thought to bring down healing rays. The absorption of this light energy is sent out by the healer for several minutes so that total saturation is effectively transmitted. There should be appropriate bonding and dialogue between healer and patient throughout this process.

The colour of the symbol is pink on the right hand side and purple to the left. This controls both brain hemispheres. The patient should be aware of the colour content so that attunement reaches its maximum. When the healing is complete, any surplus energy will flow down and out of the body, through the lower open part of the symbol. Any residual energy will be absorbed by the Earth. Since Cosmic energy carries a positive charge, this will automatically transmit healing to overall planetary well-being.

Since this healing symbol is easily memorised, having strong mind link, there is no need after initial sighting to refer to either symbol or text visually. Always see both ends of the symbol as open for the free flow of incoming and outgoing energy.

Given 23rd September 1993

Discs represent the Cosmic eye, showing within their circular form windows into other dimensions. Being electrically charged with electromagnetic energy, they pulsate at a certain frequency, becoming activated when visualization at third eye level takes place. The Disc purports to establish a dialogue of meaningful intelligent communication. You are ready now to receive its transmissions by electrical impulses which impart Cosmically orientated thought energies to the brain. The new linkage contacts axons running from neurons. The axon cabling bifurcates to receive a second additional impulse which in bridging the synaptic gap reaches molecules with additional transmissions running on new frequencies. The first routine line receives information through the usual connections. The second new line receives Cosmic transmissions only. This altered bifurcating brain wave is part of mutational change. We are making our contribution to mankind by linking to you in this way.

If we speak to you directly at this time, much of what we convey will be outside your present experience or knowledge. The moment of accepting these new concepts occurs at the moment of self realization. You are already at that evolutionary turning point. This information has been stored in your unconscious brain from the dawn of time until now. Passed on through genetically encoded DNA patterning, it has remained in a dormant state until the present time, when it is being actively awakened. You are now open to receive Cosmic frequencies, actively participating in your spiritual destiny, given the facility of converting physical energy into spiritual. This transitional change is necessary for your final cycle.

Our signals are received as an input of intelligent reasoned thought. Part of your brain has been held in readiness for these transmissions, never being used by man until now when it becomes entirely conducive to new programming. Such mutual advantage will be finally accepted at conscious levels. Strengthen your relationship with us through prayer and meditation. Accept our presence in your minds, recognising us as a contributory factor towards spiritual growth. In time you will hear our note, presently outside your acoustic range. This sound is being amplified now, transmitted to you as a vibrational impulse which is received by adjusting brain neurons. It will be experienced by many of you as heightened sensitivity. Some may register expansion in the head or ears. There may be fullness in the throat area due to expanding consciousness which has contacted the Cosmic sound frequency and desires to express it vocally. Your left brain has some difficulty in allowing full right hand brain function at the moment, interrupting sonic fullness. In time, as you open to receive the new sound, both brain polarities will allow for complete expression.

As Cosmic awareness increases, positive and meaningful integration between different Solar systems may follow. For those of you already upon this path and whose minds are opening in love and trust, the input of Cosmic transmission is greatly enhanced.

Given 26th September 1993

aster than light we make our communications within the subconscious mind. The vibratory field of Cosmic exhalations amplify into myriad thought forms which form the basis of contact with Planet Earth. Visual and acoustic signals lead to enhanced and meaningful dialogue. Using this frequency we are able to impart knowledge into your minds. Such information now being received by you was already stored within your subconscious, or sleeping brain. By oscillation of electrical impulses, this is now being activated to advance the new consciousness of mankind, so that a growing spiritual awareness takes place. Man incarnated to experience and, in the light of this total sum of experience, complete an evolutionary cycle. Although man has knowledge and has acquired learning, he has not advanced in the realization of his own spiritual identity. Much of his life span has been occupied in having or possessing, rather than contacting soul consciousness. Whilst man constantly seeks outside himself, he is increasingly unable to discover his true self or being. His lack of motivation in this direction and over many incarnations has resulted in spiritual apathy and increasing fragmentation.

Now with imminent planetary changes there has been a combined effort, on the part of those whose work it is to monitor and to chart the evolution of mankind, to assist. The link was always there, but the need to intervene was not essential until now. We are of the same lineage or Cosmic family as yourselves. We are your soul kin and counterpart. In time and with continued evolutionary elevation you will again merge with us, returning ultimately to the Logos or Source. Now we draw closer to you to uplift and to inspire you with our messages.

It is because you are at the point of entering into a new existence or dimension that we may travel to your world outside time, for we ourselves are timelessness. We enter in through the Cosmic gate, automatically aligning with outer planetary signs and energies which guide and carry us. We are re-charging certain areas of your earth with Cosmic inbreathing. This breath creates a rhythm in tune with Universal harmonics forming into sacred symbols and is both resonating and pulsating. Those who have received us may pass through the Cosmic Portal time-gate into interdimensional experience, standing within both hemispheres of heaven and earth and as co-guardians of Earth. It is their Cosmic energy which will supercharge your planet. For this time they incarnated, they are the ascended Masters, passing unrecognised and in humble guise amongst you. When they speak the Cosmic breath is emanated, all will listen to their words. Their integrity and purity of soul merit entrance into Cosmic dimensions. Standing vestured in our breath, we clothe them in our spirit to cleanse and purify the Earth. They have stood in many other times of change and need as messengers, appearing in the latter days. These are the true prophets and you will recognise them by the fruits they offer. Know that the symbolic circle is appearing everywhere upon your earth and is an indication of new Cosmic

energies, of Universal timelessness, having neither beginning or end. All matter is
ultimately contained and held within its living centre.

Given 27th September 1993

Our work is to reach the hearts of many. We wish to open your hearts by
unfolding within your being. Since we have always been a part of you, we may
speak to you now in love and trust. Our words already imprinted within your minds, may
be released and at a time when you are awakening to the Cosmic note which will resonate
through every mind. Some will hear and will emulate their own soul-note joining with
inter-galactic sound waves, and amplifying healing energies. As the third eye opens fully
you will see us in our light form. We are as myriad as the stars in the heavens. We are
carried upon winds of Universal breath. The air waves echo our vibrations. We are present
in every particle of matter, manifesting as pure energy. We have no need of names since
we are nameless. We are the changeless Cosmic heart which is at the centre of all matter as
it permanently exists. We have neither beginning or end. We are the nuclei or seed of life.
We draw closer to you now in order to save your planet from certain extinction. To free
you from the barren wasteland into which earth could spiral if dark forces are not
transmuted and permanently sealed with the light of Cosmic fire. Should the cataclysm
takes place, it will be heard initially, as a deafening tumult together with unprecedented
sound and disorder. The dissenting whisper within the heart of man will be birthed to
gradually increased crescendo, emerging as a destructive force. This negativity will cause
structure to disintegrate and fall. The earth destroyed and fruitless will lie dormant over
many years of your time. Yielding a harvest so bitter that men will weep. This is because
the soul of Earth will have departed to heal herself within the Cosmic web of inter
planetary energies. Already signs of this coming phase are all too evident. Planetary well
being is being gradually replaced by increasing fragmentation, to be drawn ever more
deeply into the spiralling vortex of destruction. During this wasteland period, no new life
will be given to man or beast, all ensuing seed being sterile. Any form procreated by
artificial processes will be grossly mutant showing variable genetic defect. Those souls
given over to dark energies will not see Cosmic light. They will view only at their own soul
darkness. This will now be manifested. As they have not attracted or grown towards light, it
has failed to grow or to consolidate within them. Admitting only darkness, they will now
view this dimension and at physical level.

The sun as it draws earth towards itself like a magnet will give rise to extremes of
heat. The fire of the sun will be withstood by those souls who have been previously
initiated, tempered and purified by its light rays. The elect will be protected, and being

covered by a great brightness and light, brought into complete safety. Those who have failed to recognise the force of this purifying light will not survive. They will perish from earth ultimately re-incarnating onto other planets, there to continue further Karmic contracting. This cycle is at the moment held in abeyance. Much depends upon the ability of man to realize his true spiritual dimension. If he follows new paths of peace and love, all will be changed. Earth will flower and man will continue to inhabit earth as a new spiritual being, becoming attuned, connecting with all living things.

Given 29th September 1993

The circular shape of the Disc acts as an energy container for electromagnetic particles. These, coupling with various combinations of protons and neurons, are charged to release changed gravitational fields which when interacting with other force fields propagate increased energy or power to affect matter. The two main parts consist of receiver and transmitter. When in connection these two components trigger each other to act as magnets, changing matter, and creating a reversal in time and space. This leads to altered states in Disc usage. If the person focusing upon the screen produces by mind thought the other complementary identical half of the magnet containing the change over point, synchronization occurs. This change of dimensional viewing is without and outside time. This is a momentarily holding, being ultimately re-released back into the appropriate channel of earth-regulated time span. Those of you able to contact Disc energy in this way gain access to Galactic Space and information.

The Disc also acts as a hologram, producing in many receivers a three dimensional image which is retained by the mind at sub-conscious levels. This is also an entry to changed dimensional states. Some of you have been unable to harness the frequencies of the Disc at this Cosmic level. This is due to present left hand brain conditioning which when in opposition or conflict with the right hand brain creates imbalance or the inability to accept new patterns of thought. This leads to fluctuation in incoming frequencies. Retuning or re-aligning helps to break down existing mind barriers. Your mind centres have already been activated to receive and transmit the new Cosmic frequencies giving the higher mind content and valid information.

You are asking who we are? We are the higher energies, composed of many variables yet focused as one source. Just as your present civilisation contains many different root races, so are we as different as the sands upon the sea shore. Just as you are unique, so are we. We stand in your time with an express purpose. We work to open channels of pure spiritual light, to encourage you to give unconditional love and light, healing all others within your path. You will realise us when the time is requisite, We are

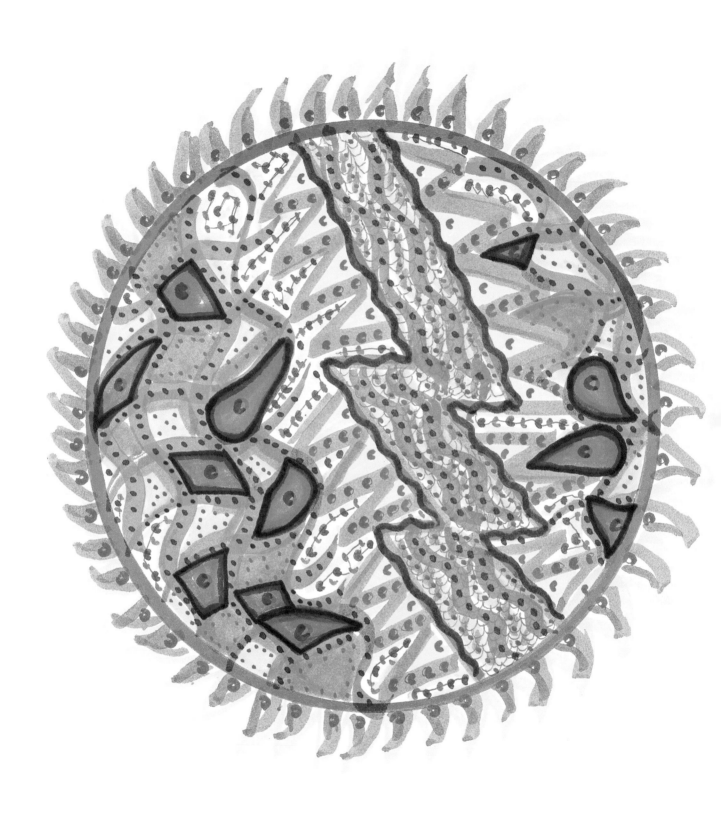

NEW COSMIC ENERGIES

constantly evolving spiritual essences poured out upon your world. We are The Cosmic Christ standing in every age of man.

Do not confuse us with many lower energies which are attracted to your planet. These present in a very different way and have no valid spiritual message to impart. For us there is no need to circle your dimension in space craft, or to disclose parallel worlds full of advanced scientific techniques. There is, however, a need for you to grow in awareness and discernment regarding some of these life forms. They often present as evolved beings offering spiritual fruits. Do not harness their energies: they are cloaked in deception. These entities cannot withstand our light; encircle them with Cosmic light - they cannot harm you. We touch you through the higher self and at the speed of light. We have no form although we may clothe ourselves in the vesture of coloured energy. We are the ever increasing light within your soul centres.

Given 1st October 1993

Men of purpose, men of vision, we speak to you in this your present cycle. Four ages have now passed upon the earth. The last and final cycle is the fifth. You are presently within this last age of man. We stand as your benefactors in your time of crisis. We speak to you as we spoke to men during the last global disaster. Such disasters have taken place on your planet many times before. When negativity reaches saturation point, there must be ultimate purification. This cleansing disperses dark energies which have accumulated over many centuries, and which lying dormant may be activated or aroused by similar energies. As negativity builds it creates a circulating wave to strongly reproduce or reinforce. This emanation cannot be dispersed unless the opposite energy is released. The final outcome is a symbolic war between the forces of heaven and earth. Such archetypes will be recognised by many of you as Michael and Lucifer. Ultimately good triumphs over evil. You now stand in the battle arena where this scene is to be re-enacted. It is necessary for the healing and cleansing of Earth, who as a living entity has become defaced and deformed by the evil which exists in the hearts of men. She has to be released from the negativity which has ravaged her over the centuries, and ultimately restored to pristine brightness.

Once long ago we spoke to the peoples of Atlantis, a proud people superior in skill and knowledge to that of your own. There were many who would not open their hearts to our words. In sadness and grief we witnessed the final holocaust in which the sea arose to engulf Atlantis which now lies beneath the ocean. The earth was then cleansed and healed. Subsequently a new land mass arose, arising from the sea as the former city was engulfed.

Few escaped from that final cataclysm. Those who did so were new beings who carried with them the promise of new life. You are their seed.

Global disaster if it comes again will be on a much wider scale than before, causing seas to rise and mountains to fall. Red hail will cover earth, falling from the sky as huge crimson stars burning and destroying all within its path. Then the Cosmic sun will appear in the heavens, to be seen by all men. Fear will tear at their hearts. All then standing as equal will be joined by the common need to survive. At that time all past civilisations will re-appear to be seen as visual reminders that the great outcome has been reached. This will occur within the fifth and last cycle of man upon Earth. Nature raising her mighty head will span the earth like an eagle spreading massive wings, to show the proud power of her unleashed elements. Then man will bow his head to pay late homage to the natural law or perish, this in the moment when he stands alone, powerless against the terror coming from the skies. Many will not stand against this final purification. They will pray for the earth to open and admit them to its fiery core. Finally the earth will be cleansed, restored and sealed to light opening to new dimensions in Cosmic space and time. This cycle will be known as heaven upon earth and is the final phasing. This global disaster is held in abeyance and may be averted even at this late hour, if man seeks peace, honouring his brother man.

Given 4th October 1993

As your conscious levels continue to develop, an unparalleled increase in extra sensory perception will occur. This will facilitate the capacity for thought energy to be projected telepathically. Most of you have experienced time travel during sleep when your subconscious mind is fully operational, and without normal prohibiting conscious mind conditioning. This is now to be recognised at conscious levels, which implies greater realisation and capacity of mediumistic abilities. This has lain dormant in most souls over many earth incarnations, mainly due to blockage in that part of the creative brain which has been denied expression, reinforced by the norms of what is and what is not acceptable behaviour.

As man continues to evolve, parts of the brain, previously unprogrammed, will now find acceptable levels of new expression We have been in communication with you through these unprogrammed areas since time began, although you were unaware of our contact, except in sleep or in the hypnogogic state. Our contact then was mainly through symbols and visual signals. These were stored within your subconscious minds until such time as they could be utilised. To those of you who were unusually receptive, we were able to speak in the visionary state. Those who received such messages were often rejected and

58

spurned by Society. This method of communication failed to reach many souls. Now we would speak to all, through both right and left hand brain, and in a medium which is totally acceptable to all Cosmically orientated souls. To accommodate these new levels there will be a sharp increase in sensitivity. This will enable the new acoustics to register realistically. The mind will act as an extra sensory telephone exchange, receiving and transmitting on several new frequencies. This telepathic faculty will be finely tuned to Cosmic transmissions.

Initially this would be experienced as growing awareness into the oneness of all living things, together with wider opening of the heart chakra, the heart energy being the main transmitter for Cosmic enlightenment. Realise that you have always been a Cosmic being. You are now accelerating in your return journey to the stars from where you issued. Your awakening now opens your spiritual centre. This opening is beautiful to us; it is like the birth of a new star. It will be as spontaneous as the opening petals of a flower touched by light. It is a wonderful process of spiritual metamorphosis in which man is changed into his true dimensional state of light.

You are moving forward. You are growing towards the light. Growth is dependent upon expression. Expression is love translated into action. Go out and heal the world in which you live. Touch all men with compassion, seeing them as your true kin. As you work to achieve this, you yourself will become illumined, enabled to realise the true perception of self which, being totally divorced from outside influences, radiates only the light within. Go in peace and joy. Remember you came to serve mankind. For this you incarnated; this was always your true purpose in universal time and space.

Given 6th October 1993

It is our wish to present you with specific knowledge pertaining to future body mutation. Understanding of this channelling will be given to all seekers on the spiritual path. All that is required initially is to read new information with an open mind; once read in this way, understanding will be given. All upon this wavelength will be given the ability to read and absorb such information without difficulty. This is due to Cosmic transmissions being fed into a new and previously unprogrammed area of the brain. Understanding here is not dependent upon learnt or acquired intelligence.

Some information will be repeated in these channellings. The second and slightly revised version should then present as totally acceptable to present left hand brain functioning. This repetition should not be seen as duplication. It is a learning process of assimilation and absorption at higher levels. The electrical signals emanating from the Disc and other Cosmic pictures are produced by light wave emission which is fed into the focused sensitivity of the receiver or user on a predetermined frequency. Brain signals unite with the electromagnetic energy of the Disc to absorb light waves, which in turn create a two way system of effective communication between Disc and recipient. This is the Cosmic telepathic system of inter dimensional communication, engendering intelligent thought and subsequent action.

This enters the etheric body as an additional understood source of energy which will stand in reserve as a back up when extra input is required. As such it becomes operational only when mutational change is strongly presenting within the physical, acting as a buffer to counteract excessive shock or discomfort to the nervous system. When released into the body stream, this energy opens the higher chakra centres to increased flow and acceleration. We have given you all Cosmic picture symbols for the express purpose of using them as working tools. They are advanced blue prints which, when used appropriately, enhance present understanding and increase conscious awareness. Such pictures have been given to man over centuries, these at certain points in his evolutionary journey when understanding and insight have been at optimum levels. They will speak with clarity and love to the pure in heart, or to those seekers of truth, imparting their information to the opening heart centre. You are coming into a cycle when all future energy will be intensified. Present fluctuational levels of energy will not be able to stand. The future body of man will be drawn up of new energizing agents, which will operate with greater efficacy. There will then be little drainage of energy levels since the body will require less by way of maintenance. It will seal energy for many years without the necessity for extra input or re-fuelling. The future sealed unit of the body will consist entirely of this new energy, which will be indestructible. In the absence of negativity there will be release from disease and death as you presently experience it. The heaviness of the physical will give way to such lightness that all in this future body will radiate with light.

Given 10th October 1993

You have long been the keepers of the Ancient Wisdom which has been passed down to each generation. This knowledge has remained stored at subconscious levels within the genetic encoding of your DNA. It has lain until now dormant, covered over and forgotten by many centuries of ignorance and superstition. Now many of you are ready to release that knowledge to those awakening with the growing certainty that they always knew and held this truth within their hearts. Connections to power or control cannot be made by these teachings. If abused or used in such a way, there could be an immediate swing to a reversal, which could prove detrimental to those not on a spiritual path.

The originating point for the Ancient Wisdom is the heart of the Cosmos itself. Each soul carries within its soul energy a tiny particle of absolute truth which is a minute reflection of the Christ consciousness. This is the entering point or connectiveness with the Source or divine ground of being which is joined to all living matter. It is ultimate merging with the Universal heart of Creative energy. Souls now opening to fifth dimensional levels will recognise their own spiritual nature and being so empowered may ultimately experience and realize Cosmic Superspace.

This vast region extending to all Universal systems and far beyond, contains the concept of timelessness and space. Being as solid as planet earth, all planetary worlds rest within it limitless boundaries. It contains the final resting place of all returning matter. It is an ever spiralling cycle of Universal breath. Within its heart lies man's journey to the stars. His ultimate knowing and realization of all that is, of being an integral part of that creative process.

As part of the earth body, you are also heir to its evolutionary pattern of change and transition. You have grown with the earth in successive time cycles. Before the mass exodus of man from this planet occurs, earth will have completed its own evolutionary cycle and transferred to superspace. This implies rapid accelerated spiritual growth for mankind at this point in time, since factors now arising have already altered present planetary patterns. Man cannot journey out into Cosmic light retaining present conditioning. He will have to seek and work towards ways of release which prepare him for his final journey. This is a period of clearing and of purification. You are the children and seed of the creative mind of God. The sacred three watch over you to ultimately free you from the chemical and animal body you presently inhabit and to elevate your spiritual nature or soul to dimensions of pure light. The world in which you live is but a third universe; as you awaken to higher spiritual dimensions you will ascend to other worlds where the chemical or animal no longer has any place. This was always the long term plan for your final evolutionary state. The disintegration of the physical will be a natural transitional process. It is not death as you have come to recognise it, rather a step into immortality. Here original thought may be experienced as man realises his true Cosmic being. Our soul is in you. Are you not always within our souls? All are one, all are connected. We send you love and light.

Given 12th October 1993

You have all carried within your subconscious minds tracings or memories of past lives. At times an overflow of these genetic patterns occurs, feeding into conscious levels and often leading to imbalance or neurotic behaviour. This is due mainly to an increased fragmentation of the self as presented at learnt mind levels, being seen as an unconnected or isolated pattern outside normal functioning. Past lives have been partially dealt with by the ongoing work of regression into those areas which have been the cause of mind disorder or dysfunction. Until now realization of the self has been unfolded through many incarnations. In many ongoing life times there will have been a repetitive theme or pattern through which the individual was required to work in order to advance spiritually and clear past Karma. Such repetition would have been strongly reinforced throughout successive lives at subconscious level, and may at certain moments of awareness or telepathy impinged at conscious levels finding ultimate expression in the overflow of previously held or contained thought. This overflow, being absorbed at spiritual levels, served to reveal man's true nature and identity. Without this knowledge or the overall realization of man's immortal nature, any spilling over of past life experience at conscious mind levels would produce only a sense of disintegration instead of the opposite experience of increased spiritual wholeness.

Subsequent lives have served to offer repeated Karmic contracting together with new opportunities to work through unfulfilled life tasks and by successful completion of such tasks complete the full evolutionary cycle. As your planet reaches beyond past Karmic laws, there will be an outstripping of all previous contracts. Man is now becoming fully aware that any past action has incurred penalties or consequences which have affected not only subsequent lives, but have also had an ongoing effect into the present cycle. Now with the completion of Karma, a new freedom will be offered which will serve to accelerate a programme in which spiritual enlightenment may be realized by many who have attained the necessary state of evolvement, this with the growing capacity to reach spiritual completion even during this life span. You incarnated at this time to participate in this programme. You are being freed to work towards the ultimate self which, being divine in nature, has always remained connected to the Source.

Being given this new wholeness implies moving away from any further need to regress the action or subsequent penalties of past lives. Any blockages resulting from the Karma of previous incarnations will now be discharged. All subsequent action should be met at present level. Your main work is now, and as long as your lives are concerned with the expression of love and service, all previous pain paths in the body will give way to an increase of healthy flow and rhythm. You are coming of age as Cosmic beings and, as you enter into this new spiritual dimension, we are full of joy and we greet you as true soul kin. We send you an increase of love and light. All are one soul, one light.

Given 15th October 1993

Many heart centres are opening at the present time. As they open there is an increase of love which supercharges, awakening all other body energies. The heart is the central point for Cosmic awakening. As it opens there is a spiritual flowering which leads to an increasing desire for union with the Source. The pulsating heart merging with Cosmic light joyously unites its resonant note, oneing to all living matter. Once heart energy is activated and the portals of the heart open to the Cosmic Sun, there is an instant recognition of man's true purpose, which consists of unconditional love and service to mankind. The heart takes on the role of seer and teacher, to convey the teaching of the Absolute. It is this pure thought which is translated into loving action. This conveys the wisdom and truth of the ascended masters who are now permanently absorbed into the Logos or Source, whence they constantly re-issue, permeating transcended heart essence into all awakened souls.

The heart, flowering, fructifies and seeds. The seeds are scattered to the four corners of the earth and, finding fertile ground in the hearts of the pure and innocent, they take root so that the cycles of fruition and harvest are repeated. Ultimately, all hearts will open to the sound and endless symphony of the Cosmic note which will reverberate in every corner of the Universe, signalling the return of all souls to the Source. This heralds the spiritual ascension of man who is now both elevated and transfigured, being spiritually uplifted, entering his new dimension in eternal space and timelessness.

This opening of the heart centre serves to encompass the ideal of service, in the light of unconditional love. The generosity of the heart is now boundless, expanding, being received and flooding into Universal space. The Cosmic heart now sees with pure spiritual awareness all that is and will be, and this contained in a single pulsating resonating beat. The heart listens rapturously to its Cosmic note which beats in unison with all vibratory energy forms to reverberate endlessly upon Eternal shores.

Once opened to light, the heart cannot close again. Its portals widen to enclose spirals of ascending love energy whose ultimate destination lies within the infinite heart of the Source itself. This quickening energy is constantly evolving in a cycled state of timelessness, endlessly issuing and returning to and from the Logos. Heart chakra energy radiating from the centre of man raises him to his rightful place within the Cosmic Order. It is through the heart that man becomes enlightened, ascending to take his rightful place as son and heir, timelessly held and united with the Source of his being. We send you an increase of love and light.

Given 17th October 1993

Your minds at present are rather like kaleidoscopes. You may feel you are altering existing patterns of previously conditioned thought to achieve overall perspective or balance. It may seem that all you have held by way of values is now disappearing, or changing, creating uncertain mind states. If you think about the workings of kaleidoscopes, you will know that to create a new pattern you have to let go of the old. A shaking up and dispersing of the particles opens to new patterns. The new pattern, always seeming to be more beautiful than the previous one, motivates you to go on shaking the moving particles to create the most desirable picture.

Your minds are now in the process of awakening to new thought. This experience and emergence of higher energies brings about the subsequent action of mind clearing. Former patterns of rigidity previously blocking new channels of creative thought are now dispersing, leaving an open entrance for the ongoing programme of Self realization, which has until now lain dormant in the minds of the majority. The expansive claiming Ego has held all together in such solidarity and restraint that freeing has precipitated uncertainty or fear. This subsequently leads to prominent left hemisphere functioning, and limits the creative right hand brain.

Entrance to fifth dimensional levels propensitates the full use of the right hand hemisphere, together with the opening of the subconscious mind. In time, and with the altered molecular structure, this new infusion will balance out to both right and left hemispheres, affording maximum optimum experience at trusting and accepting levels. Confidence is requisite throughout this transitionary phase as it serves to increase positivity, withdrawing energy from incoming negative thought patterning. It is important to allow the mind to open to new thought and experience which is independent of any previously formulated Ego valuation. This dimension can have no previous mind measurement.

This acceleration and new growth is affecting all souls at present. As the new energies are recognised and eventually harnessed in what is still third dimensional time, it may feel as though you are living and experiencing at two levels simultaneously. This will pass as integration of new fifth dimensional levels develop.

For those of you who have recognised the ongoing need for personal Guides, we say to you that you must now accept your own spiritual responsibility together with your own emerging Christ-consciousness which will stand in place of Gurus or spiritual leaders. The body you will "put on" will be the radiant light or ascended body which in time will totally eclipse the present dense physical form. The body, being completely absorbed into emissions of light emanating from the etheric or future electrical body, will become totally encapsulated into the Source itself. By its Oneing with the Source it remains an integral part of the Absolute. It is within that final dimension that it becomes enlightened.

Given 19th October 1993

Male and female energies are the wholly balanced manifestation of creation. Both join to represent the creative and sustaining forces of the universal matrix. The triangular juxtaposition of dual energies aspire towards the Source at the apex point, signifying that all energy is divine and is constantly being drawn into an upwardly spiralling state towards the divine point of being. All matter is constantly evolving by centrifugal force towards the Centre from which it originally emerged, perpetuating the Self. Its ultimate goal is to seek re-union with the Logos by its life force essence which is essentially divine by nature. Both male and female counterparts seek unified wholeness within their spiritual and cellular structure, ceaselessly aspiring towards this goal.

Every soul has now the increased opportunity to evolve, this with balance and integration of their individual gender. This purports towards full expression of the Mother-Father-God analogy, permitting full flowering of the body chalice of man which becomes his total offering to God. Here is the consummate unification of both male and female energies, activated within the Centre of Cosmic being or knowing.

The expression of love is then raised, elevated and sanctified in greater sensitive and awareness. Recognised points of giving and receiving are now highly mutable. Previous factors openly dependent upon mutual reciprocity now raise present levels towards a spiritual love which has a highly energising nature and entrance point. The focus point is unconditional love which, being outside the norm of "giving-getting", is totally selfless in expression. This permits the seed of Divine loving to germinate in fertile ground, to flower and fruit, moving always towards the ultimate and permanent unification of soul to Source.

Although the physical has always stood as the common or recognisable channel for the expression of love, there is now joined to many unions the spiritual counterpart which, being Divine in nature, elevates both partners to the emerging Christ consciousness. Many will find changed partnerships, based upon this new concept and expression of Divine Love.

The new energies encircling Earth at present have entered into many souls, vivifying and quickening, accelerating spiritual growth. The flowering heart radiates the Cosmic Sun which is the configuration of spiritual man raised to divine stature. Intensified Creative energy reveals the spiritual womb of the Source from whence all matter issues. This is the Eternal heart of love which gives life force to all souls, who will ultimately return, enriched and transfigured by repetitive cycles of previously experienced life. All then being drawn into the Cosmic breath of the Source will be breathed out again as purer higher forms of energy. This cycle is ever evolving towards the final point of total reabsorption. The heart is always the centralising point for love. When physical love is transmuted to higher levels, both male and female energies are able to integrate their complete oneness and wholeness within the Universal heart.

We send you an increase of love and light.

Given 21st October 1993

Send out powerful thought waves, so that as transmitters you may amplify beams of light energy to generate and increase fields of accumulated positivity. The electrical body is now beginning to discharge a flow or current, which, being sent out, will be strongly received by others of similar mind. This in turn when transmitted increases similar electrical magnetic fields. You will by thought be enabled to project a flow of positive energy which will create change in present disturbed conditions. These thoughts, carrying a higher energy beam, will attach to Cosmic energy. The merging of both energies combine to produce powerful telepathic broadcasts, presently at subconscious levels. All recipients receiving these transmissions will in time find them acceptable at conscious levels. They will reach out to many souls who are seeking a spiritual path.

Concentrate your thoughts at even pace within ordered and positive levels. By practising this mind discipline, subsequent transmissions will become stronger, reaching out with greater resonance to those around you. You will become infectious with the light of spirit, and souls will come to realise your empowerment. Learn how to create and hold a spiritual thought or experience by concentrating on it at mind level, touching it with mental power before releasing it to the Universe in purposeful love.

Some of you may experience initial difficulties as Cosmic energies build up. Overloading is often experienced by headache or dizziness and feelings of nausea. When these symptoms are "worked through", a feeling of increased well being follows. The "breakthrough" period will present more frequently as the energies begin to find acceptance by the physical, mental and emotional bodies, maximum benefit often following the period when energies find acceptable channels of communication at conscious mind level. The subconscious will always be receptive to such transmissions.

The new energies you are learning to harness are entirely Cosmic in origin and nature. They stream down from outer space merging with the Earth's magnetic and electrical fields. All matter becomes the receiver of this energy which radiates and charges oscillating atoms and molecules to action. This is also absorbed through the constantly spiralling movements of your molecular and cellular structure. Everything vibrates and resonates in harmony with these energies. Your vibrational and resonating fields are changing now to rapid acceleration. This is due to planetary change and future mutational patterning. You are being prepared to receive a stronger input of light wave energy which you will be able ultimately to release for the increasing benefit of your planet. There will be a new orbiting path for Earth eventually which will necessitate variation in gravitational pull. When energy transfers enough velocity to your planet, this could result in part freeing from Earth's normal gravitational pull. This is the reason for the development of the future light body which is able to function adequately, without presenting difficulty in new climatic change. The way lies ahead; there can be no point of return. This present period is concerned with adjustment, allowing you to effect any ongoing programme of transitional change at minimum level.

Given 22nd October 1993

Of the seven Master root races, man now exists in the fifth cycle. Two more cycles are to emerge, each conferring an additional sense. These two last senses are entirely spiritual in nature. The first gives transcendence over the material universe, the second permits the ascension of man uniting him to the Source. The fifth cycle will witness man's emergence into new levels of telepathic communication and expanded consciousness. A new mind will admit him to fifth dimensional experience. This is the first gateway to the stars. Man is a space being. He is a traveller in time. The planet in which he lives is a space ship journeying to timelessness. At this point in his journey, life force will be enhanced as Man begins to understand his own spiritual nature, which touches upon the point of Christ consciousness, and within his own being or centre.

As the stars in the Universe resemble points of reflected light as seen from planet Earth, so man will become increasingly aware of his own light which is a counterpart of all total Cosmic energy. He too is a star, whose light may not be put out, and will be seen by all as an earth star of great brilliance in the days of darkness. His soul star in the Galaxy retains its original brightness, burning with pure and ceaseless light whereas, until now, the light in man has become darkened, almost extinguished.

At one point in your existence, you were one with the stars, one with Cosmic light. You carried this light as a single eye, in the centre of your forehead. You knew infinite wisdom, possessed all knowledge. You and nature stood as one to balance the great Cosmic forces as they flowed into Earth. You were the bridge, the connection for such energy to flow through you into Earth at optimum level. You were then the Mediator, the Cosmic Christ. The balance was a state of Union between Man and his Source. As man developed, knowledge drew him into a state of unknowing; the pure eye of vision, the eye of seership, blurred and eventually closed. In this cycle two eyes formed and opened, bestowing upon man his present mode of visual interpretation. The third eye is now only opened when the soul reaches into the higher consciousness of the God-light. The darkness in man no longer permits him to see the earth as it really is, beautifully radiant, rainbowed with Cosmic light and unchanged. It is man's predatory nature which has closed upon that original vision and light.

There is now a point when he stands at great risk incurring total disconnection from his spiritual roots. This will lead to a loss of centredness which inevitably results in ongoing fragmentation of the Self. Soulless man easily predisposes towards a Robotic man who may be easily programmed by refined artificial intelligences. Becoming the futuristic man of iron rather than a being of light.

We urge you dear children to make the point of return so that your inner vision is clear. You will then re-awaken to your divine nature. When the balance is equal, man may indeed walk once more amongst the stars, entering into wholeness and complete unity with his Source.

Given 24th October 1993

You are the mirrors of the Universe, reflectors of Cosmic light. You act as vessels for earth revitalization. Cosmic energy is drawn into you and emanated by your breath which is the vitalizing life force. This being emitted, it merges to form part of all universal electromagnetic energy. Your polarity embraces heaven and earth, acting as a magnet to alter the vibration of incoming light waves which then find changed frequencies on many planes. The earth is continually replenished by the frequency of your individual resonance and harmonic energies.

As your vibration is absorbed into the Earth, it becomes one with its centrifugal force, feeding it with streams of electromagnetic flow. In raises spiritual levels; you are enabled to act as loving participants towards inter planetary purity and radiance. It is important to elevate these levels now, so that Cosmic energy is harnessed and at optimum strength. Many souls are generating negativity at this present time. This is received by earth as a dark inert energy, it lies dormant until reactivated by similar frequencies. This destructive force generates itself, multiplying rapidly. In many areas where this energy has prevailed, there is a resulting increase in violence. This is occurring on your planet at the present time, and the dilution of such energy is critical.

As sons of Earth, you have a clear responsibility to create a climate of peace, which in turn will feed and nurture your Planet positively. This should be your primary aim. By discharging this duty, you elevate both yourself and the Earth in which you live. Residual energy is either transformative or destructive, depending upon the quality of individual lives. The earth is also a living entity. You and your planet are irrevocably linked by mutual dependency. When your physical shell is returned to the Earth it is absorbed into the soil to be eventually used for ongoing revitalization. This repetitive cycle of birth, life and death becomes an essential part of the God-man nature worship of Earth itself. Mankind's contribution as a life form completes this unending cycle. Over many incarnations man has left Earth, giving back his physical shell to reclaim a new body, in order to fulfil previously unpaid Karmic debts. By completing many life cycles he is satisfying the primary condition of replenishing the earth together with working out his life task or purpose. If man has received, then Earth has been the giver, for his life, survival and enjoyment of a beautiful world.

Man came from the stars. He chose Planet Earth for experience; the earth in loving partnership afforded him such experience. He is indeed in debt to the Planet he presently occupies. As he has received abundantly from it so he should give again to the Earth as a true custodian and guardian. The work of healing nature is long overdue. The Earth now looks to man to restore, by love and light, whole areas which have been wasted or affected by his warring nature. He must change from his present role of predator. His energies being employed in service and unconditional love make him the giver. It is love alone which will ultimately create soul transformation. Then the flowering hour of his rightful sonship is fully realized.

Given 28th October 1993

Some of you have been asking who will return to the Source and who will elect to stay on the planet as helpers in the days of great need. This is already chosen by the soul at the time of its first incarnation and is written into subsequent incarnatory cycles. The soul-elect has undertaken to work in a particular way at that time when service to mankind will be discharged at optimum levels. Some souls incarnate infrequently having fulfilled karmic contracts within previous cycles, when their lives were exemplary and above reproach. These souls have chosen to return to Earth at the present time, free of Karma. They are already living amongst you, although many will be unrecognised. Some are ascended masters who have also chosen to be here and of service. They will stand openly visible as great beacons of light. These will call to the peoples of the world so that they are nourished and fed by them in days of great spiritual awakening. These Ascended masters stand in your time. They are immortal beings and as such are not subject to the laws of death and rebirth.

They are joined by other souls who have elected to return to Earth. These souls will remain until the end of their life cycle to assist many who will actively seek their light. These are already moving into the Light bodies we spoke of in earlier channelling. This cycle signifies for them the completion of the Karmic contract which they engaged in previous life cycles. If the spiritual climate is raised and cataclysmic events negated, these souls will then return to Source, not re-incarnating. Other souls who have already returned to Source will elect to take their place, returning to Earth, and being recalled for future service should events again necessitate this. So there are in fact many tiers of prepared and waiting souls who could reincarnate into further life cycles assisting mankind on earth, in times of unprecedented need.

Many other souls who have not yet completed their Karmic contract will reincarnate to other worlds where similar Karmic conditions prevail. We have told you that no soul will be lost. Ultimately all souls will return to the Source. For some there will be a longer period of purification and evolvement. This may require many future incarnations elsewhere.

Your own planet cannot offer you sojourn for the future. It is now tracking towards a new orbiting path which will eventually cause it to become unstable. Loss of gravitational pull will cause Earth to ascend, altering existing life forms in no uncertain way. There will be massive mutational change. Many souls will be unable to meet these changes and will give up their souls. These will transfer to another Universe which is already now in existence and is awaiting them. This earth change is part of a natural ongoing process, and will be gradual. It should not be confused with any future impending disaster which, if taking place, will be entirely due to the gross irresponsibility of man. It is our hope that such world wide disaster will be averted and that man will go forth and prosper in a new climate of love and peacefulness.

Given 30th October 1993

You must turn away from fear, so that your hearts may open to love. Create a climate of peace and trust which opens the mind towards change. Once fear is eliminated from the process of change, there is admitted a growing acceptance towards new truths and an ability to embrace them as they present within your lives. The heart opening to light permits recognition of your spiritual height and dimension. When this takes place, there is a "letting go" of all past accumulated memory experience which may have filled the system with strongly reinforced negativity. This emptying out predisposes towards a new sensitivity which is translated as uplifted tranquillity. This is often followed by a sense of release and great lightness which accompanies such a process. The physical and the subtle bodies experiencing "Ascension," harmonize to create altered states of consciousness, which reflect an overall sense of deep resting peacefulness and love. Being ultimately conveyed to the true self, this truth is then totally acceptable, finding lasting expression in acts of pure unconditional love and service. It is then that all things having touched this flame are subsequently transformed.

You are being transformed at this time in no uncertain way. Many events in your past life will be removed from conscious thought paths as though you had no recollection of them whatsoever. Such memories have been healed by love and are no longer required for re-assessment, examination or reliving. They are no longer necessary to you as past experience, or to be held by your minds as ongoing thought processes. That space being emptied of continuous replay is now able to tune into new patterns of spiritual thought. This takes the place of previously wasted energy.

The new energies are finding expression within the hearts of all those who have spiritually awakened. There will be a growing recognition of their own soul light and empowerment. As these energies continue to be absorbed, there will be a turning away from past materialistic goals, and a growing desire for spiritual growth and advancement. Change begins with the individual, following to others. You are the channels for this new change which is now being experienced in loving commitment and action. We see your energies emerging as pin points of bright light which shine in a darkened world. Soon, these points of light will merge together, and as one great flame, fuel the heart of the Cosmic Sun. This will serve as the focusing point for the new planetary light which will dispel the forces of darkness forever, drawing all things towards its brilliant radiance. Children of light we greet you always. We stand in your time as guardians of the Earth.

Given 31st October 1993

As you open to the new energies you will be enabled to deal with situations in a new and different way. Previous conditioning which has been mainly linked to ego reasoning will no longer provide you with a predictable slide rule of mind measurement. In this new light there is no existing disparity between any soul. Each person in every situation will now stand within your heart as having equal merits, and as such present to you without like or dislike, preference, blame or praise. The mind, being emptied of previously stored memory patterns which have influenced past or presenting social behaviour enactment, will now programme to new decision making, bringing all men before it in a favourable, unbiased non-judgmental light.

You will experience difficulty in closing towards any new connection which is productively active in militating towards this movement of soul-mind intention. As you relate to others in this spiritual mode, a field of abundant fruition in which you participate as garner or harvester is generated. Life force flourishes and seeds in relationships which are now based upon truth and honesty. Previous conceptions of truth become changed and re-measured within this climate. As these concepts are carried into ongoing situations and relationships, a reciprocal expansion of soul-light takes place. This is the entry point for the right hand brain polarity to express new thought processes to the left hemisphere. That programme then becomes totally acceptable to both right and left hand brain, integration leading to wholeness of being, dispelling fragmentation which has formerly served to create a divided mind.

The new spiritual clothing is light and integrity, freeing the spirit to serve with increasing compassion, love and understanding. Maximum benefits derive directly from such selfless action. Limitations being removed, likewise so are expectations. By opening to every situation at soul-heart level, there is little room for selfish speculative thought or action. Then as every door opens wide, actions become purified and love-filled. This is the beginning of individual ascension and fifth dimensional time.

The soul then standing within the centred heart of love itself is unable to express anything except that which it has received from the Source. It becomes saturated, radiant, and transfused with the essence of loving, and, reaching out to all men, covers them with the bright flame of its own soul light. In that moment it has become love, and regenerates the world.

Given 3rd November 1993

You are being empowered to speak to many souls, whose understanding of the knowledge you impart will find its way powerfully to their heart centres. Your words must be chosen carefully and with a growing sense of responsibility since the impact of the message will be strongly experienced by them. In a way you are rather like the cutting edge of a diamond, a precision tool, accurate and sharp. The slightest pressure of the diamond will mark a receptive surface with a deep and permanent incision.

There will be a growing sense of your spiritual responsibilities towards others. This will be discharged only in the light of love and honesty in your dealings with them. You are the shepherds; your flocks will have the degree of caring and love you give to yourself. This will be reflected in the quality of care you offer. Any other platform which falls below such standards will not seed or grow to fruition. One single action of unconditional love may create great change, accelerating regenerative soul-growth. This in turn militates towards a thousand fold amplified energy of pure spiritual intent which becomes a healing beam of light directed towards the forces of negativity.

This then is your main spiritual task in the present incarnation. You have been carefully prepared for a mission of service to mankind. You are entrusted with the care of many souls, bringing them into light and love. This implies a deeply generous heart, giving without thought of reward. You have in a way deliberately delayed the gratification of personal accolades, accumulating post karmic indebtedness until you return to the Source. We will always clear the way for you to fulfil this contract, although you will incur the common penalties of the human condition to which you are presently subject.

In your hand we place the two edge sword of wisdom and truth. As sword bearers you may wield its mighty power to subdue dark forces which present so powerfully in your world. As it is held aloft it creates powerful laser beams of light which destroy the growing negativity around you. As these fall away, an infusion of pure light is transmitted which darkness may not tolerate. Many seeing your light will tremble. Many will not admit you for their fear of your brightness. You are a powerful light in a dark world. Many will not awake from their spiritual torpor. Leave them to sleep, they are not your responsibility. Go to those who will receive you in love and truth. They are your flock, you the caring shepherd. Know that there is open war at this time between light and dark forces. The latter energy is strongly reinforcing itself in a last attempt to overthrow the spiritual. You will need to be stronger than you are at present to combat this growing power. It is like a huge cancer spreading amongst those souls who have embraced its deceptive message. It engulfs them and will not release them. They are rendered powerless, impotent to fight against its negative devouring nature. You are the little ones of light, you shall be made powerfully strong to stand against them. Are you not the Davids who stand against the Goliaths with purity of intent? Stand sword in hand gathering those souls to you who are also of the Light.

Given 5th November 1993

You are beginning to radiate from your centredness which is the seat of the spiritual self. This harmonizing centre is both vibrant and reflective and may be visualised by others as inner wholeness or spiritual integrity. As you are transmitting resonant energy to all who come into contact with you, there will be an exchange or infusion of reciprocal shared experience at higher soul levels. This mutual interaction will make for increased awareness of vibratory signals, which being interpreted will convey as a heightened sensitivity.

The new energy is compared with a purified spiritual breathing which at times is extremely powerful when contacted at conscious levels. There is a sense of "overflowing" into channels of new thought which appear to be outside normal function or conditioning. The ego, however, will with continued presented experience of such altered states, come to accept them ultimately, viewing them as a new compartment of the mind, and one previously unencountered. This is due to the opening of fifth dimensional levels we spoke of in earlier channellings. Sustain a state of open trusting awareness. This leads to easy entry of new frequencies or the channels designed to open and feed the higher mind with Cosmic intent.

Any noticeable acceleration or expansion here militates towards the realization of spiritual goals, and for many of you these goals will fill your minds, often to the exclusion of everything else. Great release is now being experienced, together with a powerful sensitivity which is leading into a opening telepathic faculty allowing for increased powers of communication between man and the Universe. This is not totally a psychic gift, it is the returning of the Ancient Wisdom and the subsequent re-opening of the third or central eye.

Now is the time for walking on stars! Change past negative archetypal symbols into positive present imprinting. Fear disappears as the mind begins to open, flowering and fruiting in loving confidence and trust. You are conversing with angels! Many of you are now inhaling and exhaling colour, being in tune with its resonance. Those who are sensitive amongst you will experience taste and smell in its structured energy emission. Rainbows now appearing more frequently will show great variation in shape, colour and texture. Energy may be visually contacted at colour level also. The connection between colour and sound is being fed into the new mind signals. These collective colours are the present spiritual releasing of heart essence whose powerful energy, rising far above earth, vibrates and oscillates towards the Source which in creative love gathers it towards Itself. This is soul-ascension at conscious and Divine levels, this is the sound wave and the joyful song of the creature who, finding it has wings, soars rising to enter the heart of love itself which is the Logos and its soul counterpart

Given 6th November 1993

There will be an emptying out of energies at the Solar Plexus level since these are now moving upwards towards the heart centre and combining with the spiritual essence of the heart. This creates a new power centre totally balanced, finding meaning within service and unconditional love. The higher and lower self merge, indicating a spiritual partnership which is the sign of the Initiate or disciple. Advanced spiritual states serve to reinforce their attraction, manifesting through the increase of soul-centredness.

As this soul infusion takes place there follows a deepening recognition towards the hologramic nature and wholeness of creation. This is contacted by critical focusing towards spiritual intent. Combined with the ever present threat of planetary annihilation there runs beside it, as an alternative, increasing global spiritual awareness, and all that this elevated and changed state could offer to mankind. The duality of these opposites sparks the third side of the hologram, not yet manifest, which touches out of all known perspective, offering a three sided aspect of the new systemic structure viewed simultaneously and at present reflected only within soul-states of altered consciousness. This holistic vision was at one point in man's evolutionary journey offered freely, all parts of his mind being in sharp tune and resonance with Universal forces. Man has presently closed down upon this gift, much of the brain's present capacity, retaining only that small awakened part which equips him for combat and survival. In standing closely within his lower nature, he is able to witness only a small fragment of the sum totality.

Many souls are now becoming increasingly active in recognising their inherent spiritual stature. Man, in growing away from the higher self, has merely immersed himself in the limited body of the gross physical world. He will be unable to evolve further in this incarnation if he does not free himself from this lower nature, moving upwards towards states of soul-centredness.

The present grouping of souls who are aspiring towards initiation are forming pockets of spiritual energy (light) which is positively contributing towards world peace and unity. Already their spreading light contacts the higher beings, and is seen by them as pure soul-illumination. They represent the second and emerging side of the Universal Hologram. The third and completing side will be viewed at fifth dimensional levels where outer, inner and super-space combine as one. ongoing whole. All then is viewed simultaneously within the new hologramic mind and eye of future man. The first side is completed, the second ensuing, the third and final aspect is yet to take place. This is dependent upon the degree of soul-essence released into the converging harmonic universal frequency of timelessness and space. Then it will unfold like a scroll. Many of you will not understand our words at present. We say to you that the time is coming when man's mind will open only to the truth. Then he becomes the hologram with complete understanding, seeing all things. Then there will be shown to men that which was previously hidden. Then all will shine with the radiance of the enlightened soul.

Given 8th November 1993

Changing levels in thinking/feeling have often impinged upon the ability to free yourselves from recurring expressions of old thought, which have largely influenced past experienced realization patterns relating to ego measurement. You think one thing and yet feel another which is at times, unacceptable to you by way of present mind judgement or evaluation. Conflict causes a rift or blocking, often preventing change to patterns of unwanted or stagnated thought, and leaning towards over dependency in left hand brain polarities or functioning.

Past struggles to rationally balance, or to come to terms with traumatic events have overcrowded existing memory banks to the exclusion of newly created positive orientated thought. Mind space containing large areas of unresolved conflict, which are being constantly reviewed or re-evaluated stultify uninhibited free flow and lead towards neuron displacement. This imbalance is the root cause of neurosis. Neurotic patterns serve to undermine healthy functioning, minimizing right hand brain input. inhibiting spontaneous creativity. Ultimately this polarity becomes dissociated, and partly separated from the orderly left hand brain which is given priority. The left polarity being linked to the ego strongly reinforces ongoing assessment or rationalization of unmet goals demanding requirement of unresolved conflict. This creates a network of stress which is set up within a system intolerant of its far reaching effect.

Within the new frequencies or channels there is a balance and harmony which is wholly conducive towards new patterns of healing, permitting of spiritual emergence. This state being linked to the higher self, calls for an immediate release of past accumulated negative thought debris which it sees as damaging and stress filled. Once stored fear has been cancelled, there is revitalization to the entire nervous system. The end result is an influx of peace and quiet acceptance, allowing you to "let go" of past memories which have contributed towards the impairment of healthy mind patterning. With this "emptying out" new mind space is created which has the ability and desire to absorb and conserve Cosmic thinking at conscious levels.

You are like children at the moment, caught up in a new learning process. The mind of the child is receptive and open. Your minds require that childlike quality as you receive new patterns of unprecedented thought. The subsequent ensuing action will be wholly spiritual. New learning processes require new skills, fresh goals. The skills you are acquiring now will find ready acceptance into memory banks for future ongoing referral. As the brain unites in unquestioned acceptance of new thought, old conflicts present unemotionally, fading becoming ultimately displaced. You are your own teachers now, and as your minds open there is newly contacted inner spiritual awareness and sensitivity. All you need is within you. Learn to centre yourselves and touch your inner being. You are too concerned too restless at present to enter this state except for brief moments of your given time! Listen in the silence of wordlessness. Still the mind. As this is experienced there is oneness and unison at all levels. Soul energy standing as interpreter for these new mind signals, covers them at all times with integrity and truth. You are moving towards the light, you are coming into the light with joy, with freedom, totally released and transformed into light itself.

Given 10th November 1993

The spiritual qualities of the soul are contained within the matrix of the Logos. From a single point of uncreatedness it emerges, perpetuating itself in immutable ways. Ultimately seeking to re-admit the transience of its nature by regaining permanent union with the seat of Universal energy and resonance.

You are the transmitted seed of the Source. You are breathed out from the Centre to scatter replicating, reflected particles of the Godhead. The body is the vehicle for soul experience, returning either full or empty handed. Barren incarnations do occur, where soul intention has become unintentionally weakened or distracted from its original purpose. Defying the true nature of its earth task, it then is unable to contribute towards the total evolutionary spiral, finding itself after death in void space which is representative of the embryonic tissue of soul-sleep. There it must rest until its intercessory role to return is acceptable to Universal law. Consequently this soul must return to previous cycles of completed evolutionary growth and those which were fruitful, proceeding again from this point.

Many souls who have returned to Source with their main task uncompleted have awaited years before reincarnation in further life cycles has been granted. Many still await this opportunity. To some souls, further life experience is not again given. They remain at a fixed stage of evolutionary growth. this in union with the Source, although at lesser levels. Their hierarchical banding being totally acceptable.

Most souls in this present incarnation have gathered together on earth, accepting contracts of maximum requirements, which involve greater service to mankind. Their soul experience is at initiate or discipleship level. They are here to fulfil all soul goals before returning to Source. They have passed through many stages of earth life to come into this last important evolutionary phase, realizing that this is to be their final opportunity to advance spiritually. They are also aware that there can be no further petition for return in further incarnations to this planet. This knowledge which is now being imparted at conscious levels, carries great responsibilities. They are in one sense the final Cosmic breathing or exhalation. They will be gathered to the Source in the ultimate inhalation of timeless space. This act is commensurate with the re-absorbing properties of the Cosmic grid which acts as a distributor and receiver of Universal energies.

The service you are presently required to discharge to your fellow man is heroic. There will be strong motivation when open recognition for ongoing soul advancement presents. This will grow out of individual soul-light and will be linked to the existing soul contract agreed when previously returned to the Source. The work of the Ascended Masters is now open to many souls wishing to advance spiritually at this time and no other. Know that you have chosen to serve.

Given 11th November 1993

As the consciousness opens, the stored accumulated knowledge of the higher self over past soul lives will be disclosed at conscious mind levels. This release of empowered spiritual thought takes on an essentially purposeful meaning in both left and right hand hemispheres of the brain. When this occurs there will be an outpouring of spiritual gifts, these commensurate with the individual capacity of each soul. This lively expression will enable the mind to flow in increased harmony and rhythm linking and containing all spiritual energy within the opened heart chakra. This heart essence will be fed to many, all being held as beloved children, sons and daughters, and existing within the pulsating Universal heart. Male and female energies will twine and integrate, moulding around each soul, and sealing them within the resonating web of Cosmic dimensional union.

The physical being elevated to its highest level, and combining in radiant flow with the subtle bodies, will move towards higher consciousness in total balance. The spiritual body will take up its rightful place as leader or principal, co-ordinating and nourishing by meaningful contribution to all participating component parts of that body. This will reflect man's original high standing and order. You are being led into "green pastures" your cup indeed overflowing! All you have desired spiritually is now to be given. All spiritual soul kin will attract to the light you emit. You are beloved children. These events have shaped themselves around the new energies which have been pouring into the earth for over eight years. Because you have been absorbing these energies primarily through the subconscious mind, there is now rapid awakening at consciously experienced levels. This interim period will disclose to souls who have reached maximum saturation, and who are now prepared to disclose light energy, discharging it to others.

This continuous action touches readily upon the higher chakra energy, giving rise to massive change within those centres by opening them further to increased levels of consciousness. Noticeable at first will be your heightened sensitivity to less compatible energies around you. This will cause feelings of strongly experienced disruption. Your own energy field now alerting the slightest imbalance will vibrate powerfully. In time you will be strong enough to deflect such unfavourable input. As the power centre of the Solar Plexus ascends to combine with the new heart energy, there will be comfortable integration, balancing all energy fields in loving control and neutralizing them in discerning awareness. At present the Solar plexus centre has only partially ascended. When these two energies completely fuse in love, then there will be powerful energy emission. The soul becoming totally transfused by love will draw all towards it in recognised expression of its true self.

This is the completed hologramic symbol and forms the connection of the third and final side. This was set out for you to you in our recent channellings. When this is fully completed there is entry to fifth dimensional time and space.

We stand in your time and send you love and light.

Given 13th November 1993

In previous channellings we explained the end of present Karmic contracting. Your planet will no longer fulfil the law of Karma, and is moving towards the culmination of its original karmic intent for Earth returning souls. Being released from previously imposed conditions, Earth becomes totally freed from the responsibilities of this assignment. Many of you will not re-incarnate again, returning to the Source at the end of this life cycle. Any future incarnations for earth returning souls, taking place after the planetary changes will be totally free of Karmic laws.

During this present incarnation, those souls who are now engaged in their main task of Service to mankind and who are ultimately returning to Source, will by now have cleared all past karma. Therefore any outstanding karma which that soul now incurs will be cleared during the present life cycle. This taking into account, that there is no further opportunity for Earth return, to clear outstanding accumulative karma in future incarnations.

Many of you still cling to karmic principles which were part of old encoded conditioning. You are reluctant to clear built up blocks of unresolved memory patterns which adhere to you, causing strong negativity. This creates stress factors which blocking vital life force, give rise to malfunctioning within the physical and adjoining subtle bodies. This is carrying an unnecessary burden no longer valid.

Your spiritual body is petitioning for full expression now. This body is the true essence of the soul. It cannot operate at full capacity or reach its highest degree of insightful expression until you are willing to "let go" of accumulative negative thought. You will be unable to grow towards this, or to experience the vitality of spirit it holds, until you release your own resentment. That is what you are holding onto, nothing more. This inner anger re-fuels itself, growing into ever greater proportions, stifling soul growth and capacity. In a way you need to experience a loss of memory in these negative areas rediscovering your own soul-light. You have fed yourselves upon many superfluous things, often to the detriment of your own soul development. So the spiritual has failed to emerge as the main mind mentor, allowing the persuasive ego to supplant it.

Now you are moving into the light of the Cosmos, the soul is awakening, and its energy and purity will be strongly experienced by many souls. They being thirsty for its truth, will discard all in its favour. Strong desires for soul experience will take priority. It will be seen as the point for evolutionary growth and spiritual integration. This process of purification opens the soul to new light and love. Life force becomes energized and spiritually amplified There is the new knowledge of wholeness and of touching this spiritual component just as you would touch the physical; body. The new energies acting to create awareness and total self realization.

You are being drawn upwards towards the light, standing within the strength of your own soul-light. The process of change and all it involves may be painful initially, but the final outcome is glorious. This is your true dimension. We are unable to effect such transition for you. The work must be undertaken and completed by every evolving soul. We recognise your capacity to work through this process and to emerge spiritually richer. This opportunity which lies within your present incarnation and life cycle, may not be given again.

We stand in your time to assist you in love and light.

Given 14th November 1993

The development of the new mind linking enables knowledge to be received and transmitted at interchangeable and mutually shared levels with those of you who are entering 5th dimensional states. This faculty facilitates the sharing by telepathy of specialist learnt knowledge peculiar to one or other individual. This is transmitted to another using a new frequency, rather like an air wave which carries the energy of purposeful thought, implanting the required information in the mind of the recipient. Mind linking in this way serves to connects souls of common understanding, together, and within the Cosmic web of intelligent interchangeability.

There will be no duality or personality transfer inherent in this spiritual interchange mechanism. Within the new medium of telepathy each soul retains its unique originality and soul nature throughout. The mind in telepathic engagement is held firmly within the common memory grid for a fractional moment, absorbing required information at fast sound frequencies. This is inaudible to the present physical hearing system at present.

This advanced faculty is granted to those souls whose integrity and spiritual intention is above reproach. As mind energy becomes interchangeable, individuals will possess the ability to permeate other channels or frequencies, promoting even mutual compatibility. Scanning this common pool of telepathically accessed knowledge, gives distinct advantages in all future areas of work, especially within healing. The mind ray

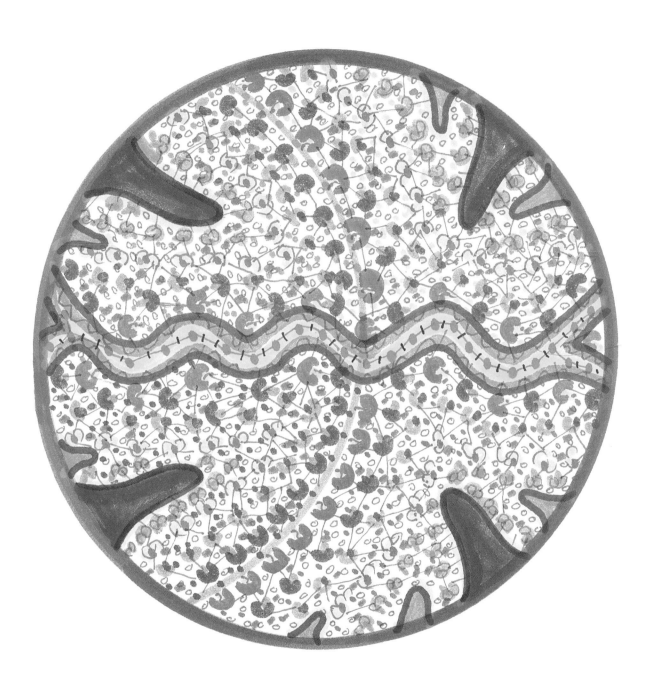

NEW COSMIC FREQUENCY

which is the telepathic component will emerge as a laser beam of silvery white light searching out and contacting skills which will moderate and rebalance at optimum level.

In time, groups will signal telepathically to other groups, sending out necessary energy by mind thought where depletion may have occurred, giving extra boosting and moderating energy levels immediately to a more accommodating balance. Where an excess of energy has been read, there will be an automatic lifting of this to a acceptable levelling. Isolated souls may be reached in this way, telepathically offering them spiritual refreshment and replenishment in days of great need. The furthering amplification of mind waves will open to these new frequencies with growing skill and increasing purpose.

Much is given to you now, for the moment of great truth when all souls will stand within their own merits, being their own Judge. There can be little valid evaluation of completed soul growth before this final epoch manifests. Many souls are now accelerating and at faster spiritual flow. They are to be given many further opportunities for greater service to mankind in the time to come, which is as yet unmarked. This serves to determine ultimately their permanent standing within the Cosmic whole.

We stand in your time with great love.

Given 18th November 1993

This is the third Cosmic Disc to stand in your time as a working tool. All are connective, serving to increase conscious levels. As you grow into Cosmic awareness, an attraction to work with these Cosmic tokens will be apparent. The seen and manifested perception of energy is new, serving to unfold by visualization, the imperceptible nature of Cosmic programming.

You will need to work with the first Disc for some time before going on to Disc two and three. The energy presented in Disc three is at a faster frequency with stronger colour encoding. The input from the Disc reaches and opens the third eye and crown chakra in those who have reached this level of spiritual unfoldment. This is essentially an informative Disc, communicating at fifth dimensional levels. All input will be retained by the higher mind and mirrored back ultimately at conscious mind level.

This Disc like its forerunners does not purport to transfer energy at high frequency after the initial bonding has taken place. The first contact and subsequent communication generally carries a higher input for a limited period. This may carry over into several Disc engagements. After a time this decreases, continuing to transmit a balance of residual energy at comfortable and minimal levels. This is to prevent any overloading, which could cause headaches or general disorientation. We would ask you to continue working with the Disc even if there appears to be little recognition of its ongoing transmission. It will continue to work with your higher mind with lessened and almost imperceptible physical intrusion.

The Disc contains the teachings of the Ancient Wisdom given in coded colour form. As you absorb this knowledge at inner levels, there will be a growing recognition of former states. This recognition may present as joyful or sad dependant upon the souls development at this phase in the evolutionary cycle. It is necessary for you to re-absorb this past knowledge which has been retained in a dormant state within the higher self, and may now be awakened and contacted for the penultimate stage in man's spiritual evolvement.

As your awareness opens fully, there will be changed recognition of the world and of yourself as an integral part of its continued evolving wholeness and identity The higher self perceiving with amazing clarity, the timeless triangular symbolism of the Cosmos-man-nature configuration. This is the entry point for fifth Dimensional experiencing which provides a viable spiritual platform for Soul Ascension.

May you increase in love and light.

Given 19th November 1993

The fragrance and soul-essence of spiritual man precedes him, spilling out and emanating from the heart as pure love. He becomes empowered, embracing all men as brothers. Now every act of loving opens the heart centre wider, flooding it with the radiance of Cosmic light. You are in spiritual touch with Universal energies now, and these will enfold you in a bright globe of white flame which purifies and burns not. This is the holy ground upon which the prophets stood. This is the transfiguration. You as spiritual beings stand within this glorious overshadowing. This fire of purifying grace consumes all which is not of the spirit. It cleanses the soul from darkness, and as you dwell within its radiance, you reflect and mirror back Light. From this spiritual womb of being, you are emitted, as warriors, clothed in great Cosmic light.

This incarnation holds the seeds of your main work or task by way of spiritual service. You are being given many dimensional gifts, the greatest being a marked increase in insight or discernment. These gifts compose the spiritual armour which is also part of the light body referred to in previous channellings. Many of you reading our words will rejoice. You will recognise them as Universal messages, which will touch upon your souls in a meaningful way, they will be as life and nourishment to you. Feed upon them and store them within your higher mind which will identify them correctly.

The new integration of mind-body-spirit imparts powerful waves of light energy which, being absorbed by the opened heart centre, create a climate of spiritual wholeness. This is then breathed out again as an amplified resonating energy which is imparted to awakening souls as new life force, functioning at higher spiritual levels. This balanced soul-state reinforces the continuing cycle and re-emergence of the God-soul-man into present time, heralding a new spiritual creation destined to walk amongst the stars and divinely linked to the Cosmos.

Your destiny is the dimension of light itself. Light worlds and the timelessness of space eagerly await your return. When the earth vehicle is finally discarded, there will remain only the joy and the ultimate experience of the ascended soul.

Given 21st November 1993

You are beginning to take on the quality of light. That light is increasing within the heart centre. Become that light for everyone you contact. Transmit its powerful rays to reach every soul. Your heart is opening now, inundated with Cosmic light you reach out to all men in loving service and compassion. The opening of the heart centre enfolds each soul in oneness with the Source, of which you are an integral part.

The invocation of the heart is silent, wordless and utterly peaceful. It is a reaching upwards, and a quiet breathing out of light itself. The soul comprehends its powerful import, conveyed at all times to existing soul-emissions. This reinforces and strengthens, giving increased distancing and advantage from those emotional and fluctuating energy centres which may have taken on heavier penalties by way of eroded DNA, and over many incarnations. These centres will gradually adapt to a more balanced and regulated overall spiritual frequency which when purifying the total body-system, will enable it to become transfused and irradiated by new and changed frequencies of restorative balance.

This growing awareness of changed soul dimension combines with the increasing recognition of your own divine origin. Begin to flow with this empowering energy which will transform all within its radius, clothing them in great spiritual light. This energy is nourished and continually replenished by the pulsating, resonating breath of the Cosmos cycle Itself.

There will be times now when you are completely silent and peace filled. Within this silence, the higher mind will sensitively listen to the sound of the Universal heart-beat. A state of enriched experienced harmony and rapport with this universal note, which is now sounding, will deepen within you, carrying over into conscious mind levels. Your own heart beat and life force merging with all soul energy of the awakened. As this Cosmic cycle is entered, there will be a strong pull towards the spiritual, whose pure energy will inundate and irradiate the subtle bodies, encircling them with the translucency of the light body even in present incarnatory existence.

Do not fear the changes which are accelerating during this present time. They are necessary for your completed cycle of evolution. All move towards, and into the infinite centre of regenerative Cosmic light. All mankind stand endlessly within that spiralling cycle of the Uncreated Source. That is, which is The Alpha and Omega, having neither beginning or end and being seated in eternal timelessness.

Given 24th November 1993

The white light of the Cosmos is paramount to the combined totality of existing star forms and presently conceived solar systems. It consists of a structureless void of intense radiation being in excess of any conceivable measurement. It is a vortex of unparalleled energy and highest frequencies. One fraction of its emitted energy could decimate entire Universes. This spiralling vortex contains the future birthing of all new Galaxies and calls forth star worlds into being. It is in a state of ever moving oscillation. It consumes and is not consumed. Cosmic worlds meet and disperse within its centre, held in suspension by the giant motion of its regulating breath. Such is the original state of the Uncreated. All things being absorbed and emitted from its centre in constant cycle. Energy into matter, matter again into pure energy.

The canopy of the Cosmos is star studded. Radiated light, trillions of light years away from your own planet Earth, highlights the incredible beauty and gigantic vastness of outer space. All stand in designated order and timelessness in compliance with the natural law which allows for its perception of reality. Behind this canopy is the Cosmic grid, generating energy in countless light wave emissions to and from all particles of existing matter. The grid is the primary centre of the One Original Energising Thought, which is the Source, or God.

This complexity regarding Creation is far beyond the understanding of the human mind. As it cannot be seen in clear totality, it is unable to be ever completely comprehended or fully experienced, excepting for its visible parts, which you have identified as your own Solar system or galaxy. Know that this vast galaxy, part of which you as man have not yet explored, is only a minute fraction of an unseen gigantic whole which completely fills total space. Space is not empty, rather full of countless atoms which are ever generating by the action of fission and creating different structural forms of matter. Everything being separated and upon separate courses, there is only friction or collision, when one or other particles of organised energy deviate from the norm. This propensitates imbalance, causing erratic movement and possible encounter with other near forms of energised structural matter.

The composition of outer space is much lighter and more distinctly separated than it is at lower levels. Within the lower spheres there is more movement and consequently greater risk of overlapping energised matter. All this is taking place in timelessness, so there can be no valid or accurate measurement by way of avoidance! This is totally outside man-time. Know that your own planet Earth was originally formed as the part result of collisive action. A huge star exploded, distributing energised matter into space. When this matter cooled at lower temperature, it formed your present Solar system. Sun, Moon and neighbouring planets of which Earth is one. Earth is attracted to the huge magnetic field of the Sun which gives it light. This light is then reflected back by Earth. Its orbiting cycle is a pull or attraction to the force field of the Sun which gives seasons and understood division of day and night. Your Earth is like a fully wound top which spins and rotates upon an axis in space. In time this planet will slow in its orbiting cycle. When this occurs there will be noticeable orbital instability, changing all present life forms as they now exist. This event may spread over thousands of years and is a phase of natural evolutionary change. This change has already commenced, but is so far gradual and almost imperceptible. This event is totally separated from planetary extinction which may be activated by the animalistic nature of man, acting solely upon his instinctual lower nature. Unless he is able to subdue this primitive part of himself and touch more closely upon his centre which is entirely spiritual, he will be unable to save himself or the Earth in which he is the voyager. We have set this out for you again and in greater detail, so that you may understand the two processes of future Earth change.

You may wonder why we have set before your minds the structure and nature of Creation. This is explained to you in the simplest of terms and serves to denote the vastness of the Universe in which you exist. Your own planet is but a mere speck in that infinite Universal order! We want you to reflect and think about space and your own part and destiny within it. Your habitat is that of a space creature. Do not take it for granted that nothing could ever destroy its status quo! Man is the proper guardian of the Earth he inhabits. His spiritual responsibility is to discharge that guardianship lovingly and with great dignity. He may only achieve that if he is aware of his own worth together with the worth of his fellow man.

May you be increasingly aware of your own true spiritual nature.

Given 25th November 1993

Know that nothing can touch you now, except the Light. Nothing can release you except the Light. Nothing can harm you if you do not accept its reality and dwell within the Light. Whatever is not of God is nothing, only a mirage, an illusion.

Everything in that sense is outside you. It has no entry unless you choose to allow it. Learn to experience from the heart centre. This is your within-ness. It is the only valid and true dimension of the self. Touch your soul in love and trust, knowing that it is as real and as close as your physical being. Reach within and experience its powerfulness. It is opening now and is sensitively receptive, attuned to Spirit at all times.

If you close your eyes, what happens? Visual signals are interrupted and the hearing becomes acute. Put your hands over your ears and the eyes are ultra sensitive. Each system tries to compensate for the other attempting to restore balance and equilibrium. All faculties when in working harmony achieve an optimum performance. The soul or centre remains undisturbed if imbalance or interruption to the physical system occurs. Being entirely independent from the connective physical there can be no required compensatory factor which changes performance. Never closing, it is at all times a centre of resonating spiritual energy. Its natural rhythm being linked to the Universal Source, it is limitless and boundless in spiritual energy. Having life after the demise of the physical, it exists both in heaven and upon earth in timelessness. It is the permanent and unchanging essence in man. The soul lives man, and not man his soul.

The world in which you live is the network of living experience for the soul. In its temporary abode, it is contained in a physical vehicle. It may dwell in many earth vehicles during its incarnatory cycles. Although the physical assembles soul experience, retaining these at conscious mind level, the majority of such earth experiences are not met at true spiritual level. The souls true and permanent enrichment comes from within and not from outside Itself! It constantly invites man to find his true centre or being within the Self. It is only when outside experience is matched to soul growth, and evaluated from that Self, that there is ongoing development and spiritual evolvement.

When the soul is slipped from the body during sleep, it moves into the higher consciousness which nourishes and sustains it. It is during this state that it has full recollection and knowledge of all previous soul existence. All is drawn together for re-evaluative assessment. It may draw upon these past experiences, recalling them in detail in order to implement the present earth cycle. During consciousness, this remains incorporated and retained at higher mind level, and is only consciously released when there is appropriate spiritual signalling.

At present there is a powerful soul linking, discharging innate knowledge. This contacts and awakens man's spirituality, by releasing heart energy and nourishing that centre which is the seat of the soul. This is the time for you to realize your own empowerment and to discharge your contract of Service to mankind.

Given 28th November 1993

BRAIN BIFURICATION

Silence fuses into a single moment of peacefulness. Peace consists in laying aside the restless, desiring mind. In this desirelessness enter the centre and the ultimate dimension of timeless space. We are part of that Centre and come to you in loving communion. When thought ceases, there is an immediate shift towards the spiritual, together with an increased longing to rest within its silence. It is only when you go beyond words, beyond action, beyond known experience and comprehension, that you enter into the kingdom of the unknown, perceiving all as one great unseen now.

Moving away from conditioned thought and its reinforcing connection opens the higher consciousness. This unconditioned mind is then engaged in meaningful communication and dialogue with the true Self, all being now outside temporal time and past-related experience. This state may be activated during meditation. There is in meditative practises an inherent emptying out of and release from prohibitive thought. This, together with a powerful drawing in of spiritual essence which unfolding within itself, manifests as the eternal womb of Cosmic awareness and Universal Creation.

The emerging seed of Cosmic consciousness is contained in such temperatures which being entirely spiritual, are consequently emptied of Ego propensity. Meditation itself is nothing more than a single act of loving. You may safely move away from organized or structured meditative practice which distracts by reason of its complexity and followed technique. You see a flower and connecting with its beauty, meditate. You see bright sunlight dappling upon a tree, absorbing its light, you meditate. Love shines from the face of a child, you meditate! You are meditating without knowing it! Taking in that soul essence and giving creative thought, priority over less worthy ones. When you are relaxed and silent, the Universe speaks to you in wonderful ways, and you reflect it then, most powerfully.

You always had the capacity to meditate! We want you to be silent and listen. You will hear the song of the spheres as they make the music of God in your heart. When the heart explodes with love, there is no reversal. That heart essence is the expressed recognition and joyfulness of the created being who is an integral part of the Creator, knowing no separation from the Beloved.

Nothing now can enter or touch you as before. It will seem as though you are distanced from events which previously filled you with such charged emotion. You will however, continue to be subject to the natural penalties and laws of Earth. There has been a great change within you, many memories have been released and you have been emptied. Difficulty may now be experienced in recalling past experiences which were originally traumatic and painful and were, at one time, deeply embedded within the conscious mind. This healing is given, enabling you to grow in love and greater spiritual freedom. Meditate upon this, recognising your enhanced spiritual ability! The new mind may more easily contact the beauty of Cosmic vision. This enables you to cross the new spiritual threshold, entering into the heart of Universal love.

Given 29th November 1993

There is an increasing knowledge of your own part in the divine plan for Earth. Rejoice then, children of light. We see the Cosmic wind blowing away the seeds of negativity. As these dark energies move away from those parts of the planet which have previously witnessed the clamouring climate of dissension and destruction, new life is emerging, together with hope for future generations. If this tide of awakening towards the spiritual germinates and flowers, there is life and not death for mankind.

Where darkness has retained strong hold, this is to be replaced by the steady influx of light which illumines the heart centres of men. As their spirituality unfolds, waves of light energy being released will inundate and flood the soul. They will stand transfigured within the brightness of the Cosmic Sun. This act allows Cosmic consciousness to reach and open the heart, which then remitting waves of limitless love will signal the advent of the new age and the spiritual awakening of the Self.

As fear recedes in the light of this transformation, you will express a new honesty and openness which translates into spiritual integrity. The fine strands of this fruitful gift, linking to the pure energy of the Source, skein to its endless radiating and cycled, oscillating emissions of reflective Light. You are being gathered to the Eternal heart of love, held and made safe within and outside the timelessness of infinite space. You are now brighter than the stars in the Universe. It is your light which will transform the world. You are become the new Saviours, the Cosmic Christs. Cosmic consciousness is opening the very doors of heaven to men upon earth!

In these times of accelerated change, there will be moments when you experience isolation. A standing alone against the massive forces of destruction. Know that during these darker moments when no light is apparent, you are always cradled, safely held, and remaining within the open heart of your increasing soul light. You will become your own protection against dark forces. They will be pushed away, destroyed by the clarity of your thoughts and intentions, which will be seen emitting from the heart centre as powerful streams of light.

The healing light you are sending out is seen by us as heart essence, its brightness rising as a clear flame to petition and intercede for your planet. This increasing force carries thought and intention upward. It spirals to and integrates with the Source whose single plan is to give life and eternal immortality to man. Your acts of love balance and merge with the heavy imbalance man has presently instigated, creating an evenness and a consistently changing state of evolving spiritual wholeness. Guardians of the earth arise, purify and cleanse with your breath all existing negativity! Claim those souls who could not ascend without your intermediary role. Recognise with great joy your ongoing commitment, knowing that you will continue to discharge this contract of meaningful service to others.

Since you are becoming light and love itself, it will appear at times that the physical container can hold no more by way of this powerful infusion. The tide of loving will continue to flow, in time giving birth to the new light body which will empower you to touch the hearts of all awakening souls. This metamorphosis is the completion of all incarnatory cycles and ongoing contracts. You are become the new Saviours, who stand in every age as light, working towards the salvation and redemption of mankind.

Given 1st December 1993

Stand within the light path of your own soul. This gateway to light is activated within you, being an illumination of the Light itself. The truth of your own empowerment is now given so that spiritual fullness may be complete. Many of you are learning in silence that going within reinforces and strengthens the soul. You are being made strong so that you may stand within your own soul light in the days which are yet to come.

The colours of the Cosmic spectrum are now clearly seen by those of you who aspire to awaken to this inner empowering. The white spectrum is a reflection of that emitted energy which, being generated by the rays of the Cosmic Sun, is poured into each heart, radiantly illuminating those dark recesses which are made transformative in love. Then all things being drawn towards this resonating energy spiral are reborn and made new within its drenching light. This saturation allows the soul to form a mystic link with the Source, completing a continuous cycle which is always in the act of ascending and descending from earth to heaven and from heaven to earth again. This soul link is being forged now and within the inwardness of absorbed seeing. This is the opening vision of Infinite Oneness, of all created and uncreated being in timelessness.

The spiritual roots you are now putting down will temper a climate powerful in light energy. This will contain you strongly within the fertile soil of the spirit. The ultimate flowering hour will finally bear fruit, to be eaten by many souls, nurturing and sustaining them in days of great need. You yourselves are nourished by us who are part of you and at the highest level. Your compassion and love will shine out in the darkness, so that all men will draw upon your light. This manifestation of the awakened spirit is borne upon the wings of the Cosmic wind, breathing new life into the hearts of men everywhere, and with powerful spiritual impact.

We invite you to extend your vision. Looking beyond recognition and realized experience of the physical body, to view limitless horizons with growing insight. You are entering now into the clarity and depth of inner perception. This is the opening and evolving third eye, which is the seat of vision, creating clarity and sharp focus of Cosmic dimensional vistas.

Your inner disposition is being strengthened in so many ways. At present much of this new transitional change is taking place at other than conscious level. In time this new change will impart powerfully-charged knowledge which will be comfortably acceptable to you all. The metamorphic process is already implanted and is taking place within you now. It is in the act of preparing you for that single and final moment of spiritual flight ,when you are to be given the total understanding and nature of the light body. In this vesture you will ascend, to touch the Universal Source and, entering into its light, ultimately become one with it. This is your soul completion and total absorption into the immortality of Cosmic dimensional experience.

Given 4th December 1993

Silence carries its own powerful charge, its sound being sensitively amplified and conveyed to the listening heart. When the frequency of this silent dimension is entered there is the beginning of instantaneous connection to Cosmic sound waves, which sweep across the threshold of the soul in pulsating rhythm, releasing the higher self to merge with the universal cycle of createdness. Within the electrifying symphony of unuttered sound is found the synchronous weave of each intertwining heartbeat of man, together with resounding revivification and connectiveness. This final Amen is articulated endlessly, emitting from the mouth of the Source in perpetuating cycle.

In sounding the Cosmic note, it frames in magnificent adoration, the wordless and swelling notes of Cosmic vibration which are purposefully expressed in pulsating colour and light. The soul in this pure state is elevated towards the final realization of knowing and being. It is consumed with the joy of the Ultimate loving. Here it would rest, opened endlessly, absorbing the music of the spheres and resonating timelessly as a soul fragment which moves silently towards all souls in perfect and peaceful alignment.

Such is the experience of the fifth Dimension which is outside thought and time itself. This dimension cannot be sought or actively awakened by the desire mind. It is totally desireless, having as its powering the essence of soul silence which precedes it. It is within silence that you will hear, and hearing will understand those unspoken messages which are given into the awakened heart. Learn to still yourselves and to enter within. The rich essence of its vibration will overflow, saturating your souls with "the love which passes all understanding."

Given 7th December 1993

Each soul has an individual note or sound. This unique vibration being released into dimensional space, resonates into patterned colour and sound as a frequency, which when formulated combines to express a geometrical whole. Your Cosmic note is continually emitted and sounding to amplify Universal energy with increasing light wave emissions. Such stimulus provides a viable platform for higher creative thought patterns which are subsequently absorbed into the Mind of the Source. The purer the vibratory note, the greater the ensuing Harmonic frequency.

Know that you are conductors of energy which is utilized in the recycling energies of the main Grid or central distributing power source. This pulsating and spiralling energy is fed into and emits from the ongoing collective energy of all existing matter. When released, this electromagnetic energy serves to power all solar systems, including your own.

Vital energy flows from the directive force of purposeful action whose single intention is ever towards the greater good. This forms a pool of usable residual energy which is never lost to mankind. Negative energy which is undirected, may also be recharged. Even this seemingly barren force field may be reclaimed and redirected to purposeful good, as this too is energy in motion. However negative energy becomes somewhat diluted and is less powerful by reason of imposed neutralization, showing a marked loss in electromagnetic properties. Focused and directive permeation emits more powerfully. This is Love or heart energy, activating a meaningful increase in the production of directional energy which is free flowing and always ascending to the Source. Its spiritual gift is in giving, on returning to Source, that individual experience which is made acceptable by soul light.

Positive vibrational thought, emanating as it does from the heart, contains the nucleus or seed of all transmitted healing energy. It is able to transform and stimulate all those within its thought path by reason of its intentional and directive activity. In purifying, the heart essence elevates towards a singleness of intention which creates integration and wholeness of spirit.

Given 9th December 1993

We listen with joy to your uplifted heart beat which is aligning to the Cosmic heart, signalling an increase in love and peacefulness. This vibratory and resonating sound reaches powerfully to merge with the Source of created and uncreated Universal energy. Then being spiritually amplified, it is returned to earth powerfully charged, entering into the hearts of mankind. This new energy is clothed in the vesture of the Spirit and, becoming the new kingdom of Cosmic awareness, grants ready access to multidimensional reality and experience.

We rejoice to see this transformation taking place within those of you who perceive the new truth. For you there will be always the growing awareness and magnificent freedom of the enlightened spirit who constantly aspires to greater soul maturity. Only when this spiritual essence is breathed freely will you absorb its innate qualities. A flame burning brightly consumes its own brightness, only within its final hour of completion does the total sum energy of that light integrate fully within the collective radiance of the whole.

As the flame is straight and always directed upwards, so you too become the new flame of Cosmic truth, illuminating the darkness of the world in which you live. Your brightness will be seen by many souls who are now made ready to accept new purifying soul light, shedding past fear and negativity, moving freely upwards and being newly born into the vision of the Cosmos which is the Source itself. As this moment of unison is realized, there will be heard the thunderous beat of all awakened hearts sounding the Cosmic note. This powerful and synchronous orchestration will break down all past experience and related thought, creating and opening to new dimensional experience. All then entering into this given Cosmic portal will shower all galaxies with unprecedented love and peaceful energy, restoring and rebalancing to pristine brightness and original first thought.

This then is the birth of the new kingdom which is the habitat of spiritual man. The purity of this illuminatory path will ultimately draw all creation towards Itself in endless tide waves of bright and burning God light. All those dwelling within this light will come to realize their own spiritual destiny, ultimately resting within the timelessness and vision of Universal heart of Cosmic consciousness.

Given 12th December 1993

All around you now are signs of earth change. These are visible in differing ways. There exists primarily a climatic shift where the seasons appear to alter, having new patterning. This will lead to irregularity and swing in temperature, noted at times as abnormal or unprecedented for the established norm. There will also occur times of unseasonal change, causing growth to emerge in unnatural cycles. Subtle changes to the magnetic energy field of the earth will affect all matter, causing world-wide disruption, violence and imbalance on a massive scale. The total sum and combination of these fluctuating energies will throw many into confusion and despair.

There may be a diminution of spiritual energy in those souls who lack stability and who are as yet insufficiently grounded. Failure to recognise the purification process inherent in all present events distinguishes them from the soul who is able to accept all events as transient or passing. There is a real need to conserve a spirit of inwardness which, being sharply focused, centralizes towards the Source and is quietly peaceful, dwelling within light .

Many spiritual qualities or gifts will be given to you during these critical times. They are showered upon you together with an increase in grace which nurtures and enriches the ascending soul. You are entering into a cycle when these are given in abundance, and with great love and trust. They are the jewels which shine brightly in times of darkness, when the forces of darkness actively militate against you, disrupting and attempting stronghold within. Be assured of great love and protection at such moments when these forces appear to prevail. They have seen your emerging light and it displeases them. Realizing the power of this light, they await with dismay its ultimate triumph. They bring with them the fruits of dark energy which are friction, stress and tribulation. There are those whose emotional centres appear to be completely powered by them.

This phase will be overcome, leading to greater spiritual freedom and expression. Distance yourselves from those men who walk amongst you, unrecognised, and lovingly accepted by you as souls in need! They will leave you always in favour of the new prophets, giving preference to the newly found and attractive! Do not feed them with your spiritual energy! To recognize them accurately there must be an increase in awareness which predisposes towards greater discernment. When this spiritual gift is absorbed, there will be instant alignment to all energy levels which will register either as compatible, or discordant and incompatible. By their fruits shall ye know them indeed!

In these days of contradiction and instability, clothe yourselves in the vesture of white light. This is a strong and powerful energy which is impenetrable. It displaces and re-aligns those emotional centres which have become excessively charged with negativity. In the future these lower centres will gradually find comfortable housing within the higher and spiritually-orientated Chakras which are becoming increasingly receptive to the heart energy. The greater your light, the more powerful its emanation. This gives less spiritual men the propensity to attack or disrupt you, as you present towards them in integrity and truth. This state of chaotic confusion is temporary and is a vital part of spiritual purification. Ultimately all attempts will be negated, and they will bring upon themselves the very energy they have attempted to unleash upon you. This is not retributive, rather the inevitable outcome of the natural law of cause and effect.

We ask you to recognise the greater need for protection at all times against these souls who have chosen to remain at static and low levels. They will reincarnate at other planetary levels to process further karmic experience. They cannot be helped by you at this point in their evolutionary cycle. Learn to conserve your energies in this direction! Your own protection must be validated. This consists of mentally standing within the light, and of becoming that light. The Master Jesus spoke of a city set upon a hill, whose light could not be hidden. You are that light which shines from out of a darkened world.

Given 15th December 1993

There is never a moment during which the soul is unaware of its Divine origins. The ongoing memory of its connection with the Source is indelibly imprinted within its spiritual eye or focus. It is at all times be-gracing itself to move upwards, towards the final realization of ultimate re-union with the Infinite. Here the full expression of the original imprinting is experienced. The dimension of the soul is unmeasured. Having neither beginning nor end, it spans time and timelessness in a single breath. It is a blue-print of the Source which is seeded into every man. In some it sleeps, in others it is awakening or awakened.

The soul exists in a dimension which is outside measured Earth experience. It is not subject or dependant upon those concepts which are purely temporal. Being fashioned in immortality, it is ageless, consisting of Absolute knowing which is the vision of God. Its completion is realized within temporary evolutionary cycles which contribute towards its final schooling and absorption into Source Light. Here it rests eternally, within the consuming flame of Universal love.

There is now a growing recognition of the true nature of the soul in many of you. This is manifested in the emerging light which declares the spiritual in man. It raises and uplifts vibrational energy to higher dimensional levels, creating divine discontent with all which does not pertain to this light pathway. It opens and releases heart essence which then overflows to uplift and illuminate the whole world.

The habitat of the soul is contained in heaven and upon earth. It has the viability to enter and exit both hemispheres as its rightful and natural domicile. This act is accomplished by virtue of the soul's permanent nature of immortality and divinity. It remains always an integral part of the Source with whom it has ongoing, continued and meaningful dialogue.

Within the network of earth experience, it chooses to retain only those truths which it perceives as validly assisting its final and designated measure of spiritual girth. Discarding all lesser thought and action, it relegates them to the seat of natural intelligence in man for final analysis, completion and selective processing.

The residence of the soul, which is diaphanous, grows from the heart centre itself which allows for its maximum expression. Actively manifested in acts of unconditional love and service, it then increases in soul-light, ultimately merging with the Cosmos Itself. The soul is the spiritual vehicle for man's journey and return to those immortal dimensions which are the declared formation and Eternal nucleus of the Source.

Given 17th December 1993

You are being given light now and in such great measure, that its influx will disperse all former darkness, illuminating and flooding the soul abundantly. This will lead to a new openness and integrity which gives growing awareness of ultimate immortality and glorious destiny. In becoming one with the Cosmic heart, the soul is cradled in love, held within its portals and light enfolded. There it rests, safely enjoying spiritual communication with the Source which nurtures and develops its spiritual nature.

Communication consists in silently understanding the Oneness of all things. This dialogue is without need of doing or saying, remaining totally outside lower-mind formulated thought processes. Its comprehension, taking in signals at higher mind frequencies, reflects only the soul-light of its own extended connection with Cosmic sources. In merging with the Absolute, it retains throughout the intactness of its own original seeding, which it recognises as the primal fragment and semblance of its union with its Creative first-thought.

The Soul cannot comprehend fear or negativity in the same way as the physical and lower mind interpret them. This is because of the frequency of these emotions present at a lower level. The soul retains its pristine brightness at all times, and is fearless. Emotional responses occurring at different frequencies are unable to affect ongoing soul transmission which, whilst retaining its original integrity, is totally impervious to those events taking place outside its centredness or wholeness.

The discerning soul is now more able to lay aside such values as are non-contributory to soul-growth and evolvement. This promulgates a new fearlessness which, lying at conscious levels, is now physically perceived. This is indicative of a growing integrity at soul-identifiable level, which serves to elevate the lower emotional response.

This emergence of new soul light, being distributed to the overall systemic whole, contributes powerfully to stand against that which purports to invade or negate its spiritual nature. Being immortal and indestructible, the soul has life in many other dimensions simultaneously. This vital life force is never dependant upon any temporal physical structure in which it may be housed. This it consistently outgrows, moving always towards its final culmination and permanency of union with the Source, which is its original point of being.

The intent of the soul is to resound its own note, merging with the full beat of the Cosmic heart which is discharging frequencies emitted as pure sound or colourless light energy. These light energies pursue their way, entering into the hearts of men, stirring souls to compassionate love and service. The heart, then opening wide causes man to weep joyfully as he realizes his divine origins. Knowledge is given in that moment of enlightenment when he aspires to nothing except his ultimate return to the Source. All now moves towards this final goal. This becomes full expression and fruition of all past, present and future aspirational thought. The soul as guardian leads man into a spiritual kingdom where his immortal nature endlessly begins.

Given 21st December 1993

At this present time we are actively supporting your hemisphere with an increase of Cosmic energy. The utilization of this gift militates towards the reclamation of those areas which are still heavily immersed in negativity. This Cosmic force is further amplified by the outpouring of the heart essence, which many souls are releasing.

We have deliberately employed this defensive strategy in order to afford man necessary time to effect long-term, positive good. We have realized over many years that your planet is gradually dying and that ,without a massive injection of soul energy, its future in the hands of mankind now stands in dire jeopardy. How may vital life source be given to this living entity which has been deprived of soul energy for thousands of years? The consequential depletion which has taken place has left your Planet denuded. Vital energy being mainly airborne is finding it increasingly difficult to penetrate your stratosphere which is becoming denser by reason of man's ongoing pollution programmes. Most of this vital input of energy is now blocked, only finding its way to Earth because of our collective and increased efforts in this direction. We are also attempting to repair critical damage to the Ozone layer. This preventative measure is now becoming an urgent expediency, controlling and curtailing unremitting output from Earth. Vast accumulated waste is forming huge toxic clouds which will eventually cause damage to other adjacent systems within your galaxy, to say nothing of your own planetary swing-back penalty. The knock-on effect here for mankind is incalculable. The ultimate responsibility is enormous!

Concentrated spiritual intention at this point in time would make for greater required contribution, which could further aid and assist the healing of your Planet. This intention may be nurtured by man only in singleness of heart and within a spirit of integrity and truth. There needs to be firm renewal and a solemn declaration of re-assumed guardianship, together with realization and committed fulfilment of that obligatory role.

Just as the inevitable outcome of war is peace, so man's ultimate benefit consists of turning away from his previous warring lower nature and of working peacefully toward the greater good of all mankind. Only by this spiritual act is he then able to effect reparation for past misuse and neglect of his planet. Only then is he totally redeemable. This must be without individual gratification or reward. Then he may gain for himself and his future descendants that restoration which will elevate him towards the Golden age of Man. This glorious age of Cosmic enlightenment and awareness was given to Man at the dawn of time. Gradually lost to sight and knowledge, the teachings of the Ancient Wisdom are held in trust for man until the time of great spiritual awakening. Then they will be bestowed once more in all their original splendour and light. As man recognises and receives with joy their immortal and timeless message, he is again born into kinship with all existing worlds and galaxies standing within and outside time. This is the final threshold of the Soul who has entered into his own Light.

Given 24th December 1993

Our links to Planet Earth have intensified since the dawn of time and man's earliest origins. As man has progressively developed over two thousand years as an earth dweller, his spiritual counterpart and inner vision have gradually decreased as he has given priority to his lower nature. He is now an unfocused entity, seeing with limited vision and insight. It has been difficult for us, in view of this, to make sustained and ongoing contact with man. In earlier days he was able to see us in our true form, our communication with him was woven into the very fabric of his existence and being. Possessing then the Corona of Absolute Truth, all things were open to him. Purposeful communication with his world drew nature and the Cosmos towards him. He was then at the pinnacle of his natural ability, existing both as man and God, permeated with Cosmic energy and possessing innate knowledge of the Source from whence he sprung, his superiority was unparalleled, unsurpassed, his vision clear and unimpaired.

Man then drawing fully upon the natural energy of the earth, held the latter in reverence. Combining earthly energy with intergalactic Cosmic forces, he dwelt within our presence in peaceful harmony. The ensuing balance created an ongoing viable interchange between the two hemispheres of heaven and earth, which were connected within and through him working at all times towards the main positive good.

As the mind of man militated against the higher self which is his divine nature, he grew away from our protection, closing to those vital messages which had previously fed and nurtured his soul. We attempted to draw closer as our transmissions in every subsequent age became weaker. The fine tuning mechanism of the Cosmic frequency was ultimately lost to man, and rendered void. As he lost contact with his higher self, he became unable to hear us. Only in altered states of consciousness were we able to regain contact with him, and then speaking to him at sub-conscious levels, stored until now, when we are allowed to speak directly to him again and at conscious levels at this time of great awakening.

The subsequent entrapping and the complex web of subterfuge into which man has presently sunk, has created a false illusion of well-being to the detriment and absence of spiritual values. It is here he has chosen until now to remain! Our present work is to reach him through this density, elevating him spiritually once more. This will be triggered within the right moment of heightened spiritual insight. Then he will be immediately restored to his original status as rightful son and heir to the Galactic Whole.

We are always part of man. That integral part being his higher self or soul. An immortal dimension whose gaze is ever directed towards the flame of the Source, and from whence all energy emanates. We are that emanation! Our responsibilities towards you are great, especially so during the present climate of great instability and change. We are permitted to draw closer to you, impregnating many of those who will admit us, with increased grace. This prompts awakening souls towards higher ideals of service and unconditional love. We stand in your time and you will presently hear us at conscious levels. We are achieving this on a completely new frequency which will become part of mutational brain bifurcation referred to in previous channelling. This developing phase becomes the germinating seed bed of spirit touching many hearts with the purity of its light flame and transfiguring all to original Cosmic awareness.

Given 30th December 1993

Your joyful return to the Source is the culminating point of all past and experienced life cycles. It is seen as the realized apex point of triangular energies which merge and form permanent union with the Cosmos. Man lying at the lowest point in this triangular configuration, elevates himself, travelling upwards during life spans towards the highest point of being which is the apex, or Source. The three sided triangle requires this unique service from man in order to create the balanced unified whole. Man supports the two arms of the symbol (Mother, Father) completing the structural diagram.(God.) He is the bridge from which the two opposite energies, male and female, spring and have their origin. It is only within this three-sided hologram that the perfected and balanced energy of Cosmic frequencies meet.

It is when man aspires to touch into his divine nature that he realizes the Apex or spiritual point of being, which is then re-absorbed into the original nuclei or seed of the Source. He then becomes the Christ consciousness, is enlightened and transcends. Then of his own volition the earth body is shed, and he assumes the radiant and immortal metamorphosis of light energy which he takes on as a positive and viable energy. We, also composed of light frequencies, support him in this final phasing as he joins to us, taking on our glorious dimension. In that moment we recognise the unsurpassable beauty of his spirit which is the developed light body. This vesture identifies him irrevocably with all transcendent matter. As he ascends, merging with all Universally purified matter, he is caught and held within the breath of the Source with divine and absolute loving.

This message is especially given for those of you who will finally return to the Source, your contract of service met and discharged. For you there is a glorious welcome as you re-enter the portal gates of the kingdom. The full realization of what awaits you here is beyond comprehension. You can have no preconceived idea of the loving heart of your Creator, who has prepared all for your return, setting this aside for the moment of joy in this ultimate and blissful moment of reunion. In your earth journey look always towards the highest star, it shines with great light for you. It is the visible apex point of the heavenly triangular configuration of which you are an integral part. Know that without man this symbolic sign could not fulfil its heavenly destiny. Man is forever part of the Universal plan. He is pointed towards the stars. To the stars he will return. Then all things being revealed he will encapsulate within the little heart of flesh, that widened spirit of the Infinite itself. Then being drawn into that mighty heart, he will dwell immortally in timeless love and endless adoration.

May the bright Sun of The Logos, illumine your souls.
Given 2nd January 1994

ow the mystical eye is opening you will see all things anew and within that field of Cosmic vision. All gifts are bestowed upon you in this day of spiritual unfoldment and awakening. You dwell always within the light of the Cosmic Sun, drawn towards its powerfully drenching rays, becoming imbued with its radiance. Its flame purifies and seals you towards the uncharted seas of Cosmic knowing. All becoming ultimately as one single fused energy or wave frequency, transmitting to Universal sources in harmonious resonating sound and colour. A single note will encompass all world vibratory levels, binding and enmeshing into the galactic web of timelessness and space.

As this new light burns steadily within, the restless ego of man recedes, and a new desirelessness is created which rests completely within the vast heart of the Logos itself. Formed of vibrational heart essence, it transmits itself towards a spiritual key there dwelling within a quietening realization of soul-stillness which signals to absolute trust and love. This love when released is overwhelming by reason of its great sweetness, breaking in waves upon the opened heart which can hold no more by way of blissful input. The floodgates break down everything except the recollection and memory of this gift, which being received in love, remains cradled within the ascending soul, that awaits its swift return.

Here the physical now, harmoniously combining, is in a state of temporary suspension. Perceiving this altered state, all systemic structure bends eagerly towards the influx of divine grace, experiencing total stillness from all former activity which could block the divine event. In so doing it contributes meaningfully towards the opening of the soul's spiritual vision. When this is infused it draws totally upon Universal love for its ongoing transmission.

What you recognise now is presently seen at etheric level only and must therefore be rightly interpreted within your own spiritual knowledge and light. In time, the etheric will be drawn down into consciousness and the physical will enjoin it, participating within its own right and with full consent and volition.

The soul is now more than ever being drawn out of its accustomed abode and keeping sleepless vigil, signals powerfully by virtue of increasing spiritual prowess, the known path of clear and directive light which eventually leads and returns it to the Source. This phase indicates the final returning path of the initiate whose ultimate desire and goal is unending union with its Creator. You bear the imprint of the initiate who is joined to such Universal matrices. You are now fulfilling the spiritual contract, becoming clothed within the lightened body which marks the symbolism of viably imparted grace.

Given 3rd January 1994

Love energy or heart essence has ethereally materialized in many souls at third eye level. This may be seen by them as a central circular disc composed of variable signalling. The colour will be predominantly violet or purple, changing from intense to paler hues and is always dependant upon the present collective and harmonic energy field of the recipient. This is transmuted from the output of higher vibrational frequencies, being stored as usable, focused and concentrated energy in healing programmes which make use of the new telepathic mind link. Energy is sent out by the healer from the circular disc as a light focused beam which when released propitiates towards former and healthier energy patterns.

It is only when you are in positive touch with your own frequency flow or resonance, that a meaningful alignment towards your own vibrational heart essence takes place. At that particular point in time, your energy sent out in love to others is able to effectively correct dissonance, accruing from opposing negative energy patterns which cause disruption or systemic disease. This is simply because heart essence, which is unconditional love, is far more powerful than any other known energy frequency.

Allow the patient to focus with maximum awareness upon the area of changed frequency which has created the pattern of stress or disharmony. Ask them to look with the eye of the mind into present dysfunction, attempting a meaningful and insightful understanding of all vital systems involved and consequently affected. Unite with the patient's thought sequence, directing a focused beam of energy from your mind into the affected area, and using the telepathic mind link to generate patterns of release through any existing disruptive frequencies. This process generates a changed flow of healing energy which, being sent out by the healer in love, reaches the patients disturbed frequency, suspending and altering former systemic imbalance. Acting as a laser, such focused energy flow amplifies higher-self energy, breaking down metabolic disturbance in existing frequencies. When this transfusion is effected, there is always relief even momentarily, from affected and interrupted energy flow.

Since this is a new gift or Cosmic faculty there must be a period of trial when this process enters into practised use. The patients co-operation is at all times requisite. Since they are active participants, maximum understanding between patient and healer is necessary. Discernment here must be at sensitive levels. Fear negates the process and patients with a iow fear threshold may be unable to benefit realistically from these new techniques. The healer should obtain maximum background information concerning the patient's level of insight before proceeding further. At all times remember the mind itself is the ultimate healer. The higher self is able to cancel out any previous disruption or imbalance to frequency fields, restoring a balanced energy at optimum and healthy levels. It is only when you are free and within your own empowerment that you stand upright.

Given 6th January 1994

Heart essence manifesting through the pineal and projected from the brow centre is rapidly developing. It is powered by Cosmic energy rays which are showered upon those souls who have contracted to work towards planetary healing and wholeness and who have elected to stand in the latter days as light workers. There will be increased skill in projecting this laser energy through the violet circular structure, which is now clearly seen and viewed through the etheric visual system. The coloured beam may be projected over distances and to any given destination. It will travel out from the brow centre in a straight and purposefully directed beam of light to reach its target.

The force of Cosmic energy which propels it is both singular and unique in its quality and properties, which are drawn from inter galactic source energies many light years away. We follow and accompany its new earth flight path, aiding its spiritual journeying. Its light/sound frequency is unparalleled, since it is fuelled by heart essence which is so transparent and heightened that it is enabled to·rise far above normal vibratory levels to reach Cosmic frequencies which support and sustain it.

For many souls the initial emergence appeared as a small disc of pure and single colour. This energy, being linked to the collective subtle bodies, transmits a resonance dependant upon changing and varying energy levels within the total human system. Depletion of life force emits paler hues, whilst optimum levels indicate deep and vivid energy imprinting. Being seen at etheric levels, it initially appeared to remain stationary at the point of its original inception. Now it may begin to move from its original positioning as many will discover its projective capacity. Projection at any given distance is realistically achieved by concentrated and focused thought energy. When this occurs the circular disc oscillates, spiralling into powerful beams of directively orientated transmission, moving forward and outwards from the brow centre.

In the early stages short flights only will be achieved. Later it will become possible, as thought becomes more positively harnessed, to lengthen the beam of the flight path, traversing space at the speed of thought. Mutual interchange will be a later development through the faculty of the telepathic mind linkage. When recalled by directive thought after journeying, it will be again rehoused and stored within the etheric at brow level. For us, this faculty has been in use over trillions of Cosmic light years and we have used it as a form of inter-galactic communication since the dawn of time itself. You see it as extraordinary, we view it as commonplace! The faculty is now to be given to those who will come to use it in great love and compassion for and in the service of awakening mankind. This Cosmic gift is one of many new faculties which are now being bestowed upon souls entering into the last cycle of incarnatory experiencing. It is drawn from the fire and flame of Cosmic consciousness which is fifth dimensional in its true and immortal nature.

Given 9th January 1994

In the last cycle, the great veins of the earth will be opened to pour out the poisonous flux of mankind which has entered and eaten voraciously into the wholeness of planetary structure. This programme of cleansing and purification is expedient to allow for a period of necessary revitalization and healing. When this phase is complete, there will be a period of resting which will postulate meaningfully towards the new change. During this phase the earth, lying barren, will temporary withhold its natural gifts or resources to mankind. This is the subsequent penalty for man's continued misuse of the Earth, becoming a natural reversal of Universal law wherein man ultimately comes to experience the bitter harvest he has sown in his total disregard of natural laws of cause and effect.

All existing matter will then disintegrate, being scattered to Universal forces which will further decimate particles within the Cosmic wind of change. Being caught up and entering into this ever-spiralling wheel of death and rebirth, original energy dispersing will subsequently re-form into particles which have been re-charged and re-energized with changed patterns of molecular structure. Such elevated structure being imbued with higher frequencies will evolve into matter which becomes more spiritually orientated towards appropriate guardianship and discharged planetary responsibility.

In this way old patterns of earth are broken up and the newer finer earth energies are consequently released to emerge with changed contracting. This continued evolutionary process forms the basis for a spiritually ascending planet which has been purged, cleansed, purified and restored to original pristine brightness and function. This new earth, reborn in resonating Cosmic colour and sound, will transcend all previous levels. The heart of man will witness the rainbowed light of the spectrum which is the nucleus of the Logos. This revitalizing partnership between man and his earth will then be pertinently re-experienced. Within this new communication, heaven upon earth will seed and fructify within the awakened heart of every living soul. Sound will amplify to a single note of praise and endless benediction. This resonant and swelling sound will reverberate endlessly, causing the fiery core of the earth to vibrate, visibly arising from its depths as a white Cosmic fire into which all matter being immersed will then re-emerge, reborn into the changed molecular structure of fully developed light bodies which are the true and final dimension of all evolving souls.

This completion of all existing soul cycles sounds the harmonic note of uniting spheres and galaxies, which merging into pure transparency of thought are consummated into eternal gazing and timelessness.

Given 11th January 1994

103

The soul graced in the experience of timelessness enters the dimensions of other worlds where it may contact its ultimately glorious state. In such moments there is significant and purposeful communion between The Logos and the soul, both being joined in deepening spiritual interchange. The meaningful dialogue which ensues bridges the gap in evolutionary journeying, spanning worlds and universes and overlapping all as one, now in a single moment of fused and blissful union.

In experiencing soul-Logos expansion, the apex point of the triangular Trinity is reached. It is then birthed, to seed and emit myriad souls of which the original and unfragmented counterpart remains singly in each one as the nuclei of the Source or point of being. This repetitive cycle being constantly breathed out is in the act of equal return. It is the ever sleepless and focused eye of Creative energy which mouths into all issued matter forming and re-forming endlessly to infinity. Since it possesses neither beginning nor end it is Uncreated energy in its constant resonating and spiralling action.

The sound of the Universal pulse is heard within the spiritual soul of man. The heart of the created beats, cradled always within the mightier heartbeat of its Creator. Its measured regulated rhythm becomes synchronized and is fully expressed within the singleness of the Cosmic note which reverberates across time and space. All then are gathered as one soul, resounding to magnificent orchestration. This is pure adoration, the love energy of which moves worlds, galaxies and universes in orbit and ordered sequence. It is the expression of the soul which becomes blissfully enlightened when in adoration it beholds the face of the Logos which is the ultimate spiritual reflection of the unchanging higher self.

The oneness of all things will become apparent, being finally returned to completed wholeness and taking on the final dimension of pure light energy. This indestructible process is the infinite outpouring of the Source itself whose single unswerving action of Love becomes fully transfigured and realized at its highest resonating point. Man has always been wholly part of this spiralling circular movement since he is an energy and as such an integral part within the universal process of soul energy evolvement. It is only when he comes to the realization of his true nature that he is able to recognise and assume the role of Co-creator, for which he has since first inception been deliberately set into the wheel and cycle of evolutionary growth. Within his final act of consummation he achieves soul completion and endless beginning, as he moves spiritually in soul-light towards total integration within the Mind of the Logos.

Given 16th January 1994

Y ou are to become the new bearers and recipients of Cosmic light. The future life flow of your planet is to be recharged by your amplified and emitted spiritual energy. This concentration of Cosmic light force is now pouring out from the opening heart centres of awakening mankind. This is the great light which will shine in the days of darkness when the natural illumination of the earth is to be withheld. Then neither sun nor moon shall give light, withholding the recognised cycle of day and night. In those days, light will be seen to emit from the radiance of the heart centre which, ascending to the brow and crown chakra region, will rest within spiritual souls. This heart essence or energy will be seen as a bright beacon whose focused rays being clearly seen will lead many souls towards the great light of the Cosmos.

Streams of energised light frequencies will cover former darkness eventually neutralizing and displacing it. All will be changed and transformed into the original light of the Source, the powerfulness of whose light path will dissolve all before its bright gazing. Planets, galaxies and Universes will dissolve and disintegrate to finally re-assemble, composed of transformative spiritual structure. This new formation of re-organized matter will be permeated by Cosmic light energy emanating solely from the Source.

In those days all souls achieving evolutionary completion and returning to the Logos will be seen visibly as ascending points of light in a sky which will take on and reflect the multicolour of the spectrum. All being caught up as one in the great rainbowed arch which has its bow permanently suspended between the recreated spiritual earth and the opened Cosmic heaven. Many will be seen to ascend, imbued and saturated with prismatic light, their transparent purity of soul revealed to all as the given light body.

The eye of the sleeper shall then be opened to look upon this wondrous sight, but it shall not be given unto him who has failed to recognise his own soul-light, this revelation leading to an ever increasing sense of loss together with the growing desire to evolve in future incarnatory cycles. The newly ascended, pouring out upon such souls their love or heart essence, will descend again to earth for a period to succour and revivify, giving new hope to those who would otherwise perish. Then the elect will finally re-ascend to integrate with the energy of the Source who is God.

In time these other succoured souls aspiring towards their individual ascension, will also take upon themselves the main task of the newly ascended in aiding the sleeping and newly awakened. This process will be repeated by all soul cycles until all are gathered into the Source, not one soul being lost.

Given 17th January 1994

Truth is stirring powerfully within the soul. As this is released former patterns of fear are eliminated. Truth frees men to seek their own singleness of purpose and intent. Double standards have contributed strongly towards distorted DNA encoding and systemic imbalance. This new light of integrity will clear the built-up debris of blocked molecular structure. Past learnt or acquired behavioural patterns are to be dissolved within the light of new spiritual values. You are moving towards new standards which deliver you from the penalties of faulty ego functioning.

New spiritual foundations are being laid which incline towards singleness of mind which evaluates situations at higher self levels. The outcome creates a sense of well-being and ongoing spiritual wholeness. This constitutes a climate in which the essence of the spiritually awakened man may flourish and grow, the genetic counterpart rooting firmly within the soil of spirit, encapsulated within the true nucleus or seed of future generations.

In your generation the implant of the new faculty may be absorbed painfully as life styles begin to deviate from the accepted norm of Society and its related expectations, former patterning often conflicting and opposing new radical thought. Present models of regulated conditioned behavioural patterns favour gain or profit rather than loss. Moving away from old prototypes upon which Society has been based for centuries in order to govern and control, will gradually erase the double standards which have always led to an increase of stress and systemic malfunction.

To use your own particular cliché, there is no longer the need to keep up with the Joneses! There is however a much stronger predisposition to acknowledge emerging spiritual light which forms a viable platform towards the establishment of this new integrity, allowing it to take a permanent hold. Although the new honesty will prove initially difficult, harnessed to future problem-solving techniques which allow and permit for fully mobile and informative action, the human ego will eventually move towards its new spiritual positioning and the reality of man's true identity become acceptably established.

Some resistance at this present time to new degrees of integrity and truthfulness may be encountered, these giving way eventually towards a new singleness of mind whose main priority is realised and met within the sole fulfilment of spiritual goals. There will be declining interest and minimum energy output towards past materialistic reach and achievement. The end result must be a sharp rise in spiritual awareness and a clarity of mind which is able to think and decide positively in favour of the individual rather than of the mass. The robotic nature of man will be eventually disarmed and changed and, as the mind clears and emerges from the debris of present media infiltration, it will then focus pertinently upon its growing empowerment.

Given 22nd January 1994

The illuminated soul shines like a jewel in the Corona of the Cosmos. Saturated by bright Cosmic rays which flood in upon its first awakening, it vibrates to Universal energy and rhythm, creating and re-creating unparalleled light beams of radiance which disclose and touch upon its divine origin and immortality.

Our unmitigated joy in the manifestation of soul awakening is immense. We stand in countless numbers around this spiritual centre of man, touching ceaselessly inwards with compassionate awareness and loving watchfulness, our vigilant guard always maintained throughout all Earth incarnatory cycles. Our main task being to ultimately return the soul greatly enriched and enhanced by Earth experience to its originating Source.

This spiritual centre possesses the potential to open flowering fully. At its highest aspirational point it begins to reflect only the light of the Cosmic sun. This takes place in moments of utter stillness and deepening communion. Then becoming increasingly and meaningfully aware, it focuses solely upon that which has given it true birth and utterance. The vibrant sounding of the Cosmic note enthrals as it remains completely centred, absorbing the oneness and unification of all things in interdimensional space and time. This phase takes place within the soul's final flowering hour. Then is the oneing of all created and uncreated seen as the ground of Divine breathing which is the pure essence of the Logos.

Since this carries the soul into spiritual completion, experience is then gathered to be finally assessed and refined. Then there is joyful recognition of the labyrinthine path which has led the soul at all times during its upward spiral, which is essentially contained within the totality of its evolutionary cycles. This is realized by the heart as a charged spirituality and wholeness, together with a marked increase in grace. Being finally ratified, this seals and beatifies all completed cycles which are then held eternally within the portals of immortal timelessness as soul measurement.

Growing separation of the soul from its Source in earth incarnatory experience imposes obstacles to growth and Divine Union together with greater distancing from the Logos. This causes pain to the soul who is eternally linked to the Logos of which it is an integral part. Much earth experience militates readily against soul growth, the ego displacing this by reason of its own materially-sought unspiritual goals. This results in continued fragmentation of the real self and imposes separation. Within the final phase the false self is ultimately displaced, giving way to the one true and permanent configuration of man's real identity as a spiritual being. As he enters into his own soul light he is then healed and whole. There is at that moment an instant recognition of his true dimension or divine being. Finally existing within this dimension, he is nothing more except the love he has finally become.

Given 24th January 1994

The mountains, trees, rivers, streams, every blade of grass and flowering kind are one with your energy. The birds of the air and the fish who swim in the great oceans are one with you. The great wastes of the Arctic, the torrid heat of swamp and jungle, the scorching heat of desert sands, these too unite with your energy. The cooling winds of summer, the searching blast of winter gales, the moisture laden rain which imparts life to all living things, snow, ice, thunder, lightning, all become as one with your energy. Sun, Moon and stars which light the Earth, these too harmonize with your energy. There is no single place or created thing on earth or in heaven where you are not. You have entered into the single energy of all created and uncreated being which is continuously held within the spiral of time and timelessness.

You move and resonate within the wheel of life which is the coloured spectrum of Cosmic consciousness. The music of the spheres is given to you within the oscillating harmonic frequency of uttered sound and unuttered silence. You are become one with the emitted Cosmic note which is the Universal pulse of being.

Now there is a fullness of joy within you as you experience spiritual wholeness. Your hands uplifted in loving benediction receive and give healing to your world. Your soul-light vibrating illuminates every particle of matter. You are become the very act of Creation itself. All then being saturated and filled, forever replenished by the energy of love. There is within this final cycle the blissful experience of completed oneness and as you enter into this oneness, you will become absorbed into the rainbowed light of the Cosmic spectrum itself as pure light. It was in this original dimension you were first breathed out in love. It is to this Source you will finally return where your opened heart will eternally to beat in unison with the great heart of the Creator.

We await your return.

Given 30th January 1994